W9-AIR-729

The End of Indexing

Six structural mega-trends that will threaten passive investing

Niels Jensen

Hh

Hh Harriman House

HARRIMAN HOUSE LTD
18 College Street
Petersfield
Hampshire
GU31 4AD
GREAT BRITAIN
Tel: +44 (0)1730 233870
Email: enquiries@harriman-house.com
Website: www.harriman-house.com

First published in Great Britain in 2018
Copyright © Niels Jensen

The right of Niels Jensen to be identified as the author has been asserted in accordance with the Copyright, Design and Patents Act 1988.

Hardback ISBN: 978-0-85719-549-4
eBook ISBN: 978-0-85719-550-0

British Library Cataloguing in Publication Data
A CIP catalogue record for this book can be obtained from the British Library.

This book is dedicated to my extraordinary wife.

Every owner of a physical copy of this edition of

The End of Indexing

can download the eBook for free direct from us at Harriman House, in a format that can be read on any eReader, tablet or smartphone.

Simply head to:

ebooks.harriman-house.com/endindexing

to get your free eBook now.

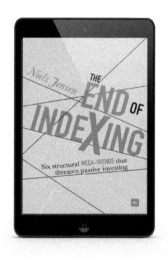

Contents

About the Author

Niels Jensen has over 30 years of investment banking and investment management experience. He began his career in Copenhagen in 1984 before moving to London in 1986. He founded Absolute Return Partners in 2002 and, today, he is the Chief Investment Officer of the firm. In 2006 he was appointed Director of a leading UK corporate pension fund, advising it on its investment strategy – a position he continues to hold.

Acknowledgements

First and foremost, I should thank my publisher, Harriman House. After having read some of my work, Craig Pearce contacted me one day in early 2016, suggesting that I could quite possibly write a book that wouldn't put everyone to sleep.

Up until that point, I had never given any serious consideration to the idea of writing a book and, at first, I was disinclined to accept the invitation – I simply had too many things on the agenda already. However, one thing led to another, and here we are. It has been quite a phenomenal experience, one that I have thoroughly enjoyed. Craig and Stephen – thank you for all the support you have provided throughout this journey.

When you write a book in a language that is not your first language, you are bound to make the occasional howler. My problem, after having lived in the UK for more than 30 years, is that I have no first language anymore. My English has never been perfect, and my Danish is deteriorating by the day – particularly my written Danish, which I rarely use anymore.

Despite some great work conducted by my primary editing team, Alison Major Lépine and Tom Duggan, a gaffe or two may still have found its way in to the manuscript, and all I can ask for is your forgiveness. Talking about working colleagues, not mentioning Shameek Patel would be almost criminal. Shameek is the artistic director of this book; he has converted all the underlying data into a series of great charts. Thank you to all of you.

I like charts – they often tell more than a thousand words – and the charts I have chosen for this book form an integral part of the story I want to tell. As most of my charts have been borrowed from various external sources, I can honestly say that this book would never have happened if it wasn't for the generosity shown by the people who have kindly allowed me access to their work.

Having said that, I ought to mention that not everyone I approached allowed me to use their work. Shame, but it only re-emphasises how much I appreciate the cooperation of those who did. Thank you so much!

As far as research is concerned, two sources stand out. Woody Brock from Strategic Economic Decisions (www.sedinc.com) has been a wealth of information in the preparation of this book. Woody doesn't pay much attention to the short term. He thinks there is far too much noise in most short-term data to draw any reliable conclusions from, which is one of the reasons I have always enjoyed working with him. Nobody provides a better long-term picture than he does. Thank you so much for allowing me to use much of your work, Woody.

Secondly, more recently I have started to work with a UK research boutique called MacroStrategy Partnership LLP (www.macrostrategy. co.uk). Like Woody, the approach to research in that firm is quite strategic in nature. They don't care much – and neither do I – why retail sales came in a bit below expectations last month. Instead, they focus on longer-term trends – an approach to economic research that I wholeheartedly subscribe to.

The whole team at MacroStrategy Partnership have been tremendously helpful when I put this book together; however, Andy Lees deserves a special mention. He has gone out of his way to help me. He has read and edited entire chapters, and his help and assistance has been nothing short of marvellous.

For example, as I wrote the passages on fusion energy in chapters 7 and 10, I very quickly realised that I was in the deep end of the pool, but Andy's expert knowledge and guidance kept me afloat. All I can offer in return is a massive Thank You.

Other people have bent over backwards in their desire to help me, but this book would probably be at least 100 pages longer, if each and every one was going to get a mention. All I can say is that your fabulous help hasn't gone unnoticed just because you haven't been mentioned on these pages.

That said, a few deserve a mention, as they did something quite extraordinary to make this book happen. Elroy Dimson, Paul Marsh and Mike Staunton, the leading lights behind Credit Suisse's *Global Investment Returns Yearbook*, Jill Mislinski of Advisor Perspectives, Ron Basu and Patrick Natale of Morgan Stanley, Chris Scicluna of JP Morgan Asset Management, and Jeffrey Passel of Pew Research Center – you all deserve a bear hug and a big Thank You.

That brings me to Leo van der Linden and Sushil Wadhwani. Years ago, the three of us worked together at Goldman Sachs. Leo continues to work there, but Sushil has since started his own company, Wadhwani Asset Management LLP (www.waniasset.com). All three of us have stayed in touch all these years, and a friendship has been formed that this book benefits from. A most sincere Thank You to both of you. Your input has been invaluable, and for that I am extremely grateful.

Shortly after I started my own business in late 2002, I was introduced to John Mauldin, who has since become a trusted business partner and a personal friend. John subsequently introduced me to Rob Arnott of Research Affiliates (www.researchaffiliates.com). I still remember how John first introduced him: "Rob raises the IQ level of any room he walks into," and he has never disappointed me! Thank you so much to both of you for your words of wisdom.

As far as the book cover is concerned, it would be grossly unfair not to mention True Design (www.truedesign.co.uk). Markus Jacob and Nick Simmons have, over the years, done a great deal of design work for Absolute Return Partners so, when I took this project on, I contacted them for their advice. When I gave them a brief synopsis of the content, I included words like *complexity, exit, perfect storm, disappointing returns* and *everything trending down*, and back came the cover you hold in your hands today. Thank you so much.

Last, but certainly not least, a massive thank you to my wife, Anne, who at times had to cope with a very distracted husband. If you have never written a book yourself, you probably wouldn't know this, but I can assure you that, when you take on a project like that, it literally takes over your life – you eat it, you drink it and you sleep it, and your poor wife is the one who pays the price. However, as these lines are the very last ones I write, I can assure you that your husband is back.

Preface

Everything is trending down. GDP growth, productivity growth, workforce growth, the rate of inflation – all are on a downward trajectory and, consequently, interest rates keep falling, and equities are running out of steam. It goes without saying that, by making this observation, I have chosen to disregard the cyclicality of the economy. Interest rates will obviously continue to move up and down, as they react to the cyclical forces of the economy, but the longer-term trend is firmly down.

The cyclicality of the economy is not what this book is about, though. The focus is strictly on six structural trends. When the debt super-cycle reaches the end of the road, when baby boomers retire in large numbers, and when a large proportion of the workforce in advanced economies begin to suffer from declining living standards, there is most definitely a root cause. One of the objectives of this book is to find that root cause.

By writing this book, I hope to raise the overall knowledge level amongst investors; help them to understand what is truly happening, why the next few decades are likely to present plenty of challenges, but also why I think we have an environment in front of us that is perfectly navigable, as long as the investment strategy is adjusted accordingly. To continue applying the same techniques and methodologies that have worked so well for all of us in the bull market of the last 35 years will most likely not lead to good results.

You may ask the reasonable question: Why write a book about trends that many of us already know will happen? *Because* I find that most investors' knowledge level about those trends is surprisingly superficial; *because* I find that few investors have seriously considered how those trends will affect economic activity and financial markets in the years to come, and *because* those trends in conjunction have the potential to create conditions resembling the perfect storm.

Few investors would disagree that something is not quite right. Why else would GDP growth continue to disappoint despite extravagantly low interest rates? That said, the same investors often fail to understand precisely why that is. Slowing economic growth is not at all the post-crisis phenomenon it is often portrayed as. GDP growth has slowed every decade since the 1970s, and that is the topic of chapter 1.

In chapter 2 I look at the big conundrum. Why on earth have equities done so well in recent years despite everything trending down? QE (quantitative easing) is often credited as the main reason why investors have had such an appetite for equities in recent years but, as you will see in chapter 2, other dynamics have driven equity prices higher as well.

Chapter 3 goes into more detail on the first of the six structural mega-trends I will review in this book – *the end of the debt super-cycle*. Since World War II ended, we have piled on layers upon layers of debt. If anyone expected (and I did) the financial crisis to put an end to that, they must be bitterly disappointed. Private debt has admittedly fallen in some countries since 2008, but total debt has risen significantly almost everywhere. I will explain why it simply cannot continue and what is likely to happen next.

In chapter 4 I dig deeper into the second mega-trend – *the retirement of the baby boomers*. Although pretty much everybody knows there is bad news down the road as far as demographics are concerned, I am often astounded by how little attention the subject gets, particularly after we witnessed how much damage demographics did, and still do, in Japan. Of the six mega-trends, this is probably the most significant one.

Chapter 5 deals with a trend that has moved to the front of my radar screen more recently. It wasn't even included in the early drafts of the book, but I quickly realised it is too important an issue to leave out. *The declining spending power of the middle classes* is the name I have assigned to it, and it is about how declining real incomes in the developed world is affecting consumer spending. It is a trend that is affecting two-thirds of all households across developed economies, and over 90% in the worst affected countries; hence the impact on economic growth is substantial.

In chapter 6 I take a closer look at Asia. *The rise of the East* I call it. It was very tempting to call this trend *the rise of emerging markets*, but I am not (yet) convinced that South America will fully participate in the success story of Asia, although I hope it will. As far as Asia is concerned, there is no question that, in the years to come, it will enjoy a strong rise in living standards. I will consider how that is likely to affect us all.

In chapter 7 I switch my attention to energy and look at what I call the *death of fossil fuels*. Based on the spectacular bear market in oil prices in 2014–15 it may be hard to believe, but the world is running out of cheap oil. Not that many years ago, the Middle East could deliver an almost unlimited amount of oil at a very reasonable price, but not anymore. On the flipside, the emergence of the shale industry has established a ceiling that didn't exist only a few years ago. On top of that, I add the concept of *exergy*, which you may never have heard of before. The logic behind exergy is also at least partly why everything continues to trend down.

Chapter 8 covers a trend that is a theme more than a trend and, in many ways, could quite possibly turn into the endgame of the Global Financial Crisis. *Mean reversion of wealth-to-GDP* is the name of this trend/theme, and it is probably the most poorly understood of all the structural trends I review in this book. The Great Bull Market, which took off in the early 1980s, generated exceptional returns to investors – not only in an absolute sense but also relative to any other period in history. In the long run, wealth *cannot* grow faster than GDP (or vice versa). Wealth-to-GDP will therefore have to mean revert – it is only a question of when.

I change gear in chapter 9, where the aim is to assess how all those trends will interact. When will they begin to impact financial markets (if that hasn't already started to happen)? And, most importantly, how big an impact can one realistically expect? I will argue that the six mega-trends I have discussed in chapters 3–8 have the potential to happen (broadly) simultaneously, and therefore could be akin to the perfect storm.

In chapter 10 I will look at ways to improve productivity. Is there anything on the horizon that could save our bacon? Anything that would make productivity grow more briskly again? Although I am very confident that the structural trends I discuss in this book will all unfold in the years to come, there are indeed a few things out there that could at least reduce the impact. I conclude that one thing in particular could fundamentally change the storyline, but I will keep that little secret to myself until we get to chapter 10.

Chapters 11 and 12 are the two concluding chapters. Chapter 11 looks at things from a more theoretical point of view, whereas chapter 12 is the investor's guide to the environment I see unfolding over the next few decades. Appreciating that things are rarely black or white, I assess the most likely consequences of the forthcoming cascade of structural trends, and I conclude that some countries will most likely muddle through, whereas others will not.

As you make your way through the book, you will note that many of the charts I use are based on US data. I should stress that this book is not US centric *at all*; however, many of the trends I discuss are better covered statistically in the US. Fortunately, it matters not a great deal, as all the structural trends in this book are global (or near global) in nature.

If certain trends are likely to affect certain countries more than others, I will do my best to point it out. One of the best examples is ageing, which is a much bigger issue in Europe than it is in the US, although one shouldn't ignore the challenge facing our American friends. Take Germany, a country with about 81 million inhabitants today. 50 years from now, the population of Germany will have dropped to about 70 million. Such a dramatic fall in numbers will have a serious impact on *everything*.

Introduction

> "I guess I should warn you, if I turn out to be particularly clear, you've probably misunderstood what I've said".
>
> — Alan Greenspan

The end of indexing?

INDEX-TRACKING IS UNDOUBTEDLY the flavour of the day. Its share of total dollar volume is now in the neighbourhood of one-third of the total US mutual fund market – a market share that continues to grow almost exponentially, and informed sources expect index-tracking mutual funds to have captured more than half of total funds under management within a handful of years.[1]

With that growth rate in mind, why on earth do I believe the end of indexing is nigh? Well, admittedly, the title for this book was chosen to provoke slightly, but only slightly. Of course, I don't expect index-investing to disappear altogether. For many years to come, index funds will remain part of the menu investors can select from when making their investments; however, I firmly believe investors will soon begin to realise that the investment environment we are entering is entirely unsuitable for index-tracking strategies, and that they will begin to exit what they have all piled into in recent years.

My logic is based on a combination of structural trends that I have identified over the years. I distinguish between shorter-term tactical

---

[1]   Source: *Financial Times* (2017).

trends, which are either cyclical or behavioural in nature, and longer-term structural trends.

The former I try to address with the decisions I make virtually every day. Will oil prices be affected by the latest OPEC agreement? Will the US dollar rise despite many investors already being very long USD? Those sorts of questions are tactical in nature and are obviously important; however, they are not the subject of this book, which will focus on the various structural trends that will affect economic growth for many years to come; structural trends that will be almost impossible to avoid.

Let me caveat what is to follow by saying that the six trends below are only the structural *mega-trends* I have identified. In addition to those mega-trends, there is also a host of structural *sub-trends*. I will not go into any level of detail in this book when occasionally referring to one of those sub-trends.

I should also point out that I would *never* claim to have figured it all out. Just because a structural mega-trend is not mentioned in this book, does not at all imply it doesn't exist. I could quite possibly be guilty of not having spotted it yet.

With that in mind, the six structural mega-trends that I believe will shape our future are:

1. The end of the debt super-cycle.

2. The retirement of the baby boomers.

3. The declining spending power of the middle classes.

4. The rise of the East.

5. The death of fossil fuels.

6. Mean reversion of wealth-to-GDP.

Before I go into a more in-depth discussion about those six trends, I should add a few important points.

Disruption – another structural mega-trend

I am often confronted with the question – why is automation not on your list of structural mega-trends? Although automation is indeed a very important trend, it is in fact only a sub-trend. Over and above that floats a mega-trend I call *disruption*, which I added to my list of structural mega-trends days after handing in the first draft of this manuscript to the publisher.

After some consideration, I decided not to write a chapter on disruption. It is admittedly a massive trend, likely to have a dramatic impact on just about everything; however, I need to understand the ramifications better. For example, why do the disrupted sometimes end up on the winning side? An example of that would be music royalties, which has been disrupted by streaming. However, despite being disrupted, the music royalties industry has doubled its growth rate from about 3% annually to 6%[2].

As far as automation is concerned, I need to better understand whether an increased use of advanced robotics is likely to lead to higher unemployment. Historically, technological advances have always been good for job creation, but automation is admittedly more significant than anything we have ever seen before in the world of technology.

If unemployment escalates because of rising automation, how much will the decrease in consumer spending hold back the rise in productivity? That said, given the demographic outlook, could exactly the opposite happen? Could a shrinking workforce hold the upper hand during wage negotiations, as robots cannot replace retiring baby boomers quickly enough? If the workforce hold the upper hand, how much could inflation rise?

Also, could robots be the saving grace for the ageing societies across Europe? Could robots man the manufacturing floors in Bremen and Stuttgart, if the Germans no longer want migrants to do the job? Could a rise in automation drive wealth-to-GDP even higher? If wealth-to-

---

2   Source: Kobalt Music Group.

GDP equals capital-to-output, and a growing use of robots requires huge amounts of capital, could it be that that the long-term stable nature of wealth-to-GDP is a thing of the past?

Disruption is something we have all been familiar with for many years. An early example of disruption would be digital camera innovators disrupting Eastman Kodak's traditional camera business. That said, disrupters are not always successful. It is a misconception that entrants are disruptive by virtue of their success. Success is not built into the definition of disruption.

Looking ahead, disruption can only intensify, and automation is only a subset of disruptive innovations coming our way. Yes, driverless cars are not that many years away, and robots will soon be able to do what humans have done for centuries; however, there is much more to disruption than advanced robotics.

For example, think Amazon and think about the extensive damage it has done to retail businesses all over the world. Before long, they may do to banks what they have done to retailers in recent years[3].

There are many questions to be answered before I could write extensively on disruption, but rest assured; I will dig a little deeper in chapter 10, and automation is very much part of my research programme for 2018, so stay tuned.

The common denominator

If there is a common theme running across all my structural mega-trends, it has to be our limited ability to affect any of them. They are all virtually set in stone. Take *the retirement of the baby boomers*. There is little that can be done about ageing. Yes, we can work a few years longer; hence we can slow down the impact a declining workforce will have on economic growth. Or we can do what Mrs Merkel did in 2016,

---

[3]   In early summer 2017 Amazon announced plans to begin lending to small businesses.

when she allowed hundreds of thousands of refugees into Germany, but there is little appetite for that in most countries nowadays.

It is therefore virtually guaranteed that ageing will negatively affect economic growth and financial markets for many years to come, and I could say precisely the same about most of the other structural trends that I will walk you through in this book.

One last comment before I start. Several times throughout this book, I state that capital that could have been used productively, i.e. to enhance GDP growth, is instead used to service existing debt, i.e. it is used unproductively.

You should read observations like that metaphorically. Strictly speaking, not every penny that is used unproductively is used to service existing debt. Capital used to service the elderly is also (at least economically) an unproductive use of capital. So is much of the capital going into the property market (think of the buy-to-let boom in the UK).

History has shown that the lower interest rates are relative to prevailing GDP growth, the more capital is misallocated (i.e. used unproductively). One could even argue (and economists are increasingly doing so) that what is effectively slowing everything down these years is a *massive* misallocation of capital.

I have even come across the argument that central banks should discontinue their practice of inflation targeting. Inflation is low for a number of structural reasons, and low policy rates do more harm than good now, a decade after the mayhem of 2008. Policy rates should instead be driven by to what degree capital is misallocated, or so the critics argue. Anyway, more on that subject in chapter 11.

When summing up all the observations and conclusions I am about to share with you, it is indeed hard to be overly optimistic about economic growth going forward. A number of structural trends that we can do little about will hold back the global economy and, when economic growth is pedestrian, corporate profitability can only disappoint.

Unless investors would suddenly be prepared to pay ridiculous earnings multiples for equities (and why would they?), low corporate profitability leads to modest equity returns. All this has led me to conclude that the broader equity indices are more than likely to deliver disappointing returns in the years to come. Simply put, investors need an entirely different approach to investing. Index funds will no longer do the job.

1
The Declining Everything

The world we wake up to every morning is so different from the one many of us grew up in. Take inflation – something that in my childhood was as certain as the sun rising every morning; however, you cannot take it for granted anymore. Come to think of it, there are many things you cannot take for granted anymore. I look at why that is or, at the very least, I begin to scratch the surface in my search for answers.

Why we are slowing down

EVERYTHING[4] IS SLOWING down. Economic growth is in a multi-decade decline. Productivity growth is losing momentum, and has even turned negative in some countries. The same goes for workforce growth. Inflation turned into disinflation at first but, more recently, the F-word of economics – deflation – has popped up in more and more countries.

What on earth is going on?

---

4   By "everything" I am referring to a wide range of economic indicators. At the same time, I note that it is not only in the world of economics things are slowing down. Formula 1 cars are not as fast as they once were. Neither are commercial aircraft!

Ever since the Global Financial Crisis nearly took us all down, financial commentators and research analysts have spent a lot of time trying to explain to a puzzled financial community why economic growth remains pedestrian, why inflation is so low, and why interest rates are stuck in the quicksand.

An endless flow of research papers has addressed the subject, collectively blaming many causes. I shall not list every single reason I have come across over the years; suffice to say that the following six reasons – or some variety of those – probably cover most that I have seen:

1. A statistical mirage

Argument: There isn't a problem. Smartphones replacing cameras, etc., underestimate actual economic growth.

2. A hangover from the Global Financial Crisis

Argument: Severe financial crises make recovery from a downturn even more difficult.

3. Secular stagnation

Argument: Reduced population and workforce growth, lower prices for capital goods, and the nature of recent innovations (e.g. online shopping replacing brick and mortar shops) all hold back economic growth.

4. Slower innovation

Argument: The pace of innovation has declined; almost everyone now benefits from the things that matter the most to productivity – e.g. electricity and transportation – and recent innovations are more marginal in nature in terms of economic benefits.

5. Policy missteps

Argument: An increase in government spending combined with tax hikes (which is a policy pursued by many governments in recent years) has had a strong negative impact on private investment spending.

6. Abusive behaviour

Argument: Abuse of market power, monopoly status, etc., have contributed to the slowdown in wages and output.

None of those six suggestions provide a satisfactory explanation for the stagnation conundrum, though. They have all played a role – some more than others – but not one deserves to be credited as the main reason.

The facts

To fully understand what is going on, I suggest you take a good look at the following four exhibits (1.1.1–1.1.4). As you can see, GDP growth, in both nominal and real terms, productivity growth and inflation have all trended down for a very long time – by most accounts since the 1970s – so something very fundamental must be astray.

Exhibit 1.1.1: Nominal GDP growth by decade (compound annual growth rate, CAGR)

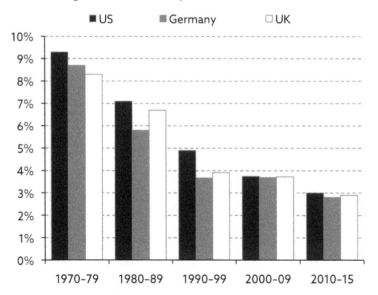

Exhibit 1.1.2: Real GDP growth by decade (CAGR)

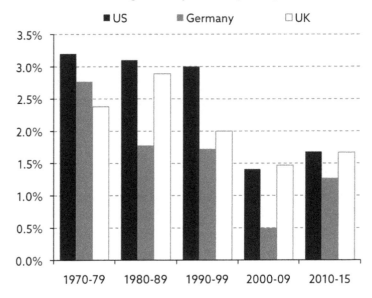

Exhibit 1.1.3: GDP growth per hour worked by decade (CAGR)

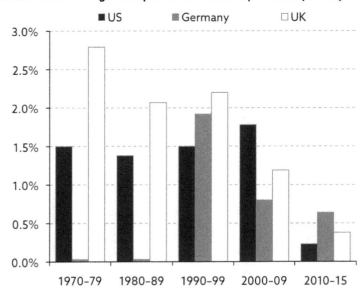

Exhibit 1.1.4: Average annual inflation by decade (CPI)

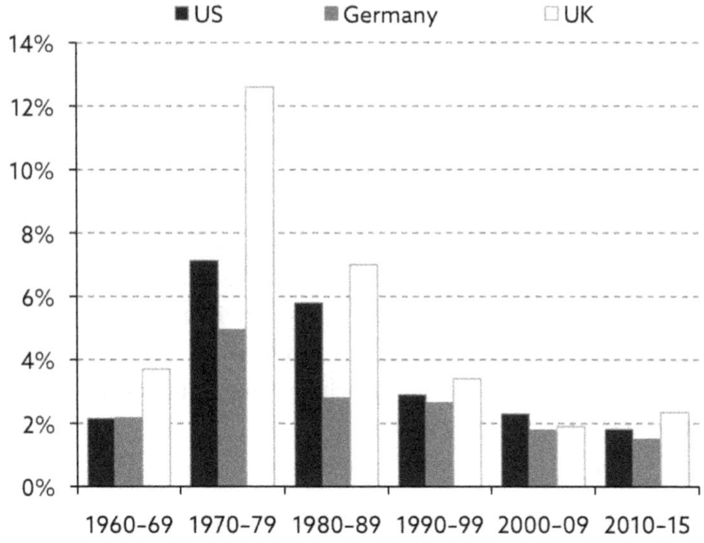

Source: Strategic Economic Decisions (2016).

A very simple way to measure GDP growth

Let's begin our journey with something very basic.

What is it that drives economic growth?

At the most fundamental level, economic growth is driven by only two factors – the total number of hours worked on an aggregate basis and the output per hour, the latter of which is effectively a measure of how productive the workforce is.

There are no reliable statistics for the total number of hours worked, but thankfully the workforce put in roughly the same number of hours from one year to the next, so the size of the workforce[5] is a good proxy for the number of hours worked. The relationship can be expressed as follows:

---

5   As per international standards, the size of the workforce is calculated as the sum of all those between the age of 15 and 64.

$$\Delta GDP = \Delta Workforce + \Delta Productivity$$

JP Morgan Asset Management has tracked how much the two components have contributed to GDP growth in the US over the last 60 years (exhibit 1.2)[6] and, as one can see, US workforce growth has been in decline since the mid-1980s.

Meanwhile, productivity growth, as measured in exhibit 1.2, confirms the picture from exhibit 1.1.3, i.e. that the decline in productivity growth is of more recent date. Both of those charts are based on labour productivity, which is the measure of productivity that most focus on; however, there is a problem. Labour productivity will rise sharply if sufficient money is spent on new machines, but that doesn't necessarily improve overall economic efficiency.

Consequently, the concept of total factor productivity (TFP) was conceived. It is calculated as the percentage increase in output that is not accounted for by the changes in the volume of inputs of capital and labour. In other words, TFP is a measure of what share of increased productivity can be explained by factors other than growth in labour or capital.

Over the past half century, almost two-thirds of the growth in TFP can be explained by technology improvements. It is a better proxy for an economy's return on capital, but it wouldn't be fair to simply replace labour productivity with TFP. They are two very different measures of productivity. Furthermore, and as you will see over the coming chapters, declining TFP growth is also one of the main suspects when looking for answers as to why everything is slowing down.

---

6   Although exhibit 1.2 relates specifically to the US, the slowdown in workforce growth over the past half century is virtually global (ex. Africa).

Exhibit 1.2: Drivers of US GDP growth, 1957–2016

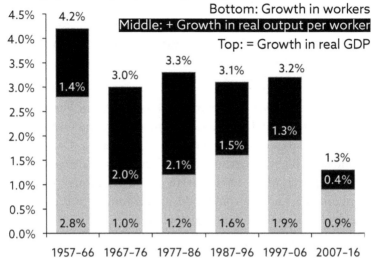

Source: JP Morgan Asset Management (2017).[7] Copyright © 2017 JP Morgan Asset Management (UK) Limited.

---

7   This material is not a product of the Research Departments of JP Morgan Asset Management (UK) and its affiliates ("JPMAM") and is not a research report. Unless otherwise specifically stated, any views or opinions expressed herein are solely those of the authors listed, and may differ from the views and opinions expressed by JPMAM's Research Departments or other departments or divisions of JPMAMs. This material is not intended as an offer or solicitation for the purchase or sale of any financial instrument. In no event shall JPMAM be liable for any use by any party, or for any decision made or action taken by any party in reliance upon, or for any inaccuracies or errors in, or omissions from, the information contained herein, and such information may not be relied upon by you in evaluating the merits of participating in any transaction.

Why GDP growth will remain subdued for years to come

Since World War II we have enjoyed only two periods of extraordinarily high productivity growth. The first was a 10-year period from the mid-1950s to the mid-1960s, where productivity benefitted from a boom in infrastructure spending.

President Eisenhower had returned from the war in Europe only a few years earlier, and had noticed how quickly the German army could move around on their network of autobahns. Consequently, the interstate highway system was established. Coincidentally, airports popped up everywhere, as civil aviation became a common mode of transportation, and you could suddenly get from A to B much more quickly. A transport revolution took place.

The second uplift to productivity materialised around the millennium, where the technology revolution – digitalisation, etc. – had a major impact on GDP growth. The internet arrived, many processes were digitalised, and we went mobile.

In both instances, productivity rose 2–3% annually. This provides us with an important piece of information. When new advances are made, whether in infrastructure, technology, or elsewhere, one shouldn't expect productivity to suddenly grow *dramatically* faster than it usually does.

For many years to come, we know reasonably precisely how much the workforce will change around the world. Only significant changes to the retirement age or to migration policy can upset those forecasts.

In Europe, the outlook for workforce growth is especially bad (exhibit 1.3), even if the true horror story is not entirely obvious from the numbers in exhibit 1.3. The worst period to come is the 20-year period from 2030 to 2050, where the European workforce will shrink the most. Consequently, European economic growth, short of any major productivity boost, will not fare particularly well between now and 2050.

Exhibit 1.3: Expected growth of various age groups in working-age population, 2010–30 (%)

Increase in the size of age groups in working-age population, 2010–30 (%)

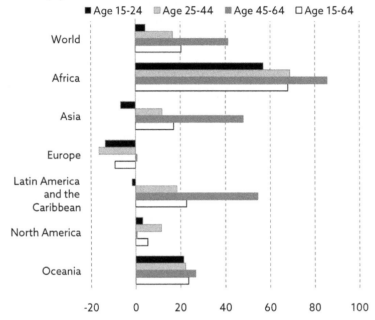

Source: The Economist Intelligence Unit (2015).

The OECD countries that will be most negatively affected by a shrinking workforce are not European, though. Japan and South Korea will both fare even worse. Both of those countries will see their workforce decline by about 1% annually between now and 2050. Negative GDP growth is therefore likely to become a recurring theme in those two countries, unless productivity can grow faster than it has done in the past.

Even in the US, where the workforce is projected to grow by approximately 0.25% annually between now and 2050, GDP growth will be modest in magnitude. Productivity gains have historically been more difficult to achieve as the workforce has aged, so the fact that the US workforce will indeed age for many years to come suggests to me that recent productivity gains of about 1% annually is probably the high end of what can be expected over the next 10 years or so.

In other words, average annual US GDP growth is not likely to exceed 1.25% over the next decade. Not impressive, but still superior to anything that can be expected in any other OECD country.

Other productivity dynamics

Estimates made on this basis are long-term in nature, though, and nothing prevents the economy from growing rapidly in a particularly buoyant year. One would have to look across at least one complete economic cycle for my estimates to stand the test of time. Think of my GDP growth estimates as trend growth estimates.

Major productivity improvements could upset this picture in a significant way (much more about this in chapter 10). As mentioned earlier, productivity is measured either as labour productivity or total factor productivity (TFP). The latter is the correct way to look at productivity when assessing the return on capital in an economy.

High levels of indebtedness affect productivity negatively, as capital that could otherwise be used productively is used unproductively – to service existing debt. Productivity growth therefore suffers not from one but from two counterproductive undercurrents: ageing and high indebtedness. I will discuss those two investment themes in more detail in chapters 4 and 5 respectively.

In that respect, low interest rates, in particular when low relative to the level of GDP growth, encourage banks to lend more and borrowers to borrow more. When money is cheap, a significant percentage of new capital is misallocated, i.e. it generates a return below the cost of capital. Capital that is misallocated causes productivity growth to shrink, i.e. one could argue that low interest rates in fact drive productivity lower.

There is no doubt that the growing use of advanced robotics will have a positive impact on productivity growth and hence on GDP growth in the years to come (see chapter 10 for more on this). That said, I would warn against excessive optimism. The counterproductive undercurrents will continue to hold back GDP growth for a long time to come.

Because of that, economic growth is likely to disappoint over the next few decades. The demographic picture is somewhat more positive in the US than it is almost everywhere else, which should allow US GDP growth to accelerate again between the mid-2020s and the mid-2030s. However, in Europe, dark demographic clouds will turn economic growth into a very subdued affair until 2050.

The consequences of low GDP growth

If GDP growth remains subdued for all those years, there are at least two important implications:

1. government policy must change; and

2. equity valuations must be reset (downwards).

As far as the first point is concerned, I shall provide much more colour on the topic in chapter 5. Suffice to say for now that we have likely reached the end of the road as far as monetary policy is concerned. Policy makers need to have a long look at the tool box and see what else can be brought out.

On the second point, there are in fact two reasons why equity valuations must come down. The first one is the straightforward link between GDP growth, corporate profitability and equity returns. If economic growth is comparatively low, so is corporate earnings growth, which again is likely to affect equity returns.

The second one is murkier. As researchers at the Federal Reserve Bank of San Francisco have discovered, there is a close link between demographics and equity valuations. As a country's average age increases beyond a certain point, equity valuations drop, and there are indeed significant demographic headwinds in the US until the mid-2020s (and much longer elsewhere) – but more about that in chapter 4.

One final point on the link between demographics and equity valuations. As you will see in chapter 4, equity valuations should (theoretically) be under much more pressure now than they are; the reason they are not is probably QE (quantitative easing). QE has distorted normal market mechanisms and has kept risk assets at valuation levels that can't be justified from a fundamental point of view, but more about that in chapter 2.

2
The Big Conundrum

Having just established that everything is trending down, and has been doing so for years, one may wonder why equities have done so well in the aftermath of the Global Financial Crisis. In this chapter, I will look for possible explanations. I will introduce the wage Phillips curve, and I will explain why a flattening of that curve to a significant degree is responsible for the solid performance of equities in the post-crisis era. Likewise, I will examine to what degree automation can explain the robust performance of equites.

Long-term average returns

BEFORE I GO into more detail as to why it is prudent to prepare yourself for more modest equity and bond returns in the years ahead (which I will do in chapters 3–9), let's briefly review what those returns have been historically.

From 1900 to 2016, real (i.e. inflation-adjusted) returns on global equities have averaged about 5% annually, whereas global bond markets have delivered average annual returns a tad under 2% in real terms. However, returns vary a great deal from country to country (exhibit 2.1).

Exhibit 2.1: Real returns on equities, bonds (local currency[8] in %)

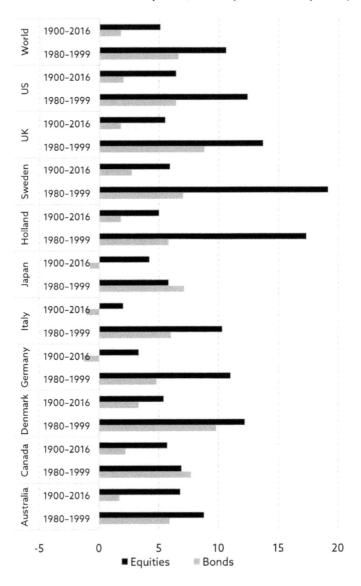

---

8   World index in USD.

Here is the problem. The majority of investors suffer from recency[9], i.e. they think of the bull markets of 1982–2000 and 2009–2017[10] as the norm and ignore longer-term return patterns. Global equities have delivered low-double digit annual returns during those two periods, and many countries have done even better than that, which is quite unrepresentative of the longer-term returns.

An entire generation of investors have never experienced bear markets to last for long and assume that central banks will do whatever is necessary for the bull market to return. Now, let me share a little secret with you. Negative real returns can persist for an awfully long time (exhibit 2.2), and there is absolutely no reason to believe it could never happen again.

Exhibit 2.2: Longest runs of cumulative negative real equity returns (number of years)

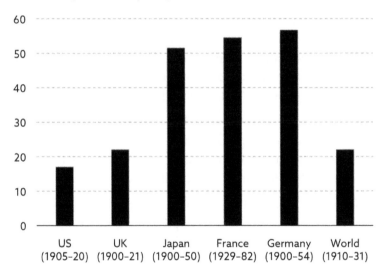

---

9   Recency is the term that describes the human inclination to assign a higher value to more recent events than to more distant ones.

10   At the time of writing this chapter (late 2017), the bull market in equities is still very much intact, and it is anybody's guess when it will be over.

Two world wars are at least partly responsible for the extended run of negative returns in France, Germany and Japan, but what is also obvious from exhibit 2.2 is that, even if you were diversified to the umpteenth degree (i.e. invested across the world), there has still been a 22-year period that has delivered negative real returns on a cumulative basis.[11]

Secular bull and bear markets

As I have learned over the years, after an extended bull run in equities, there is always an extended bear market lining up. Investors have named these long trends secular bull and secular bear markets respectively. Since 1877, we have been through six secular bull markets and five secular bear markets (exhibit 2.3).

The key characteristic of a secular bull market is rising P/E (price/earnings ratio) multiples, whereas multiples fall in secular bear markets. Furthermore, total wealth in society tends to rise significantly in secular bull markets, whereas it stagnates or even declines in secular bear markets. Over the years, there have been many more bull (and bear) markets than secular bull (and bear) markets, and the reason is simple.

A bear market is established when the equity market is down at least 20% from its previous high, whereas secular bear markets are much longer term in nature. It is not unusual to have several bull and bear markets embedded in a single secular bull or bear market.

The Great Bull Market of 1982–2000 is *the* secular bull market of all time. All three major components of private wealth – bonds, equities and property – increased significantly in value during those years, leading to an unheard-of rise in private wealth. In the US, where the access to data is best, private wealth rose by almost 8% per annum, and I am sure the rest of the world wasn't far behind. So much wealth was created in the Great Bull Market that total wealth rose to an

---

[11]   Returns in successive years are cumulated geometrically, and the total adds up to the cumulative return.

unprecedented 4.8 times GDP in the US, but more about that in chapter 8.

Exhibit 2.3: Secular US equity bull and bear markets since 1877

Year	Market Milestone	Percent Change	Number of Years	Annualised Return, No Dividends	Annualised Return with Dividends (%)
1877	Low	–	–	–	–
1906	High	396	29.3	5.1%	10.1
1921	Low	−69	14.9	−7.5%	−2.0
1929	High	396	8.1	21.9%	28.4
1932	Low	−81	2.7	−44.9%	−41.2
1937	High	266	4.7	32.1%	38.7
1949	Low	−54	12.3	−6.2%	−0.8
1968	High	413	19.5	8.8%	13.3
1982	Low	−63	13.6	−7.0%	−3.0
2000	High	666	18.1	11.9%	15.3
2009	Low	−59	8.5	−9.8%	−8.1
Now	-	172	8	N/A	N/A

Source: Advisor Perspectives (2017,1).

Americans' love affair with the Fed

There are no two ways about it. American investors have an obsessive love affair with the Fed. Anything the Federal Open Market Committee (FOMC) does is rewarded by investors, and I mean *anything*. In fact, they don't need to do anything at all. As long as an FOMC meeting is held, investors get carried away.

Before 1982, the days on which the FOMC convened were just like any other day in the US equity market, but that changed with the arrival of the Great Bull Market. Since 1982, a full one quarter of the total cumulative return on US equities has been delivered on those eight days a year the FOMC have met, *regardless* of whether interest rates have been lowered or not.

Any reason why investors changed their behaviour that particular year?

It was indeed the start of the Great Bull Market, and the Fed (under Volcker's leadership) had just won a major battle against inflation, possibly changing the perception of the Fed in the eyes of the average investor.

Even more noteworthy, in the first few years following the Global Financial Crisis, the performance of the S&P 500 on the days that the FOMC convened was no less than 29 times higher than the average daily return (exhibit 2.4).

In other words, the sheer presence of those meetings has had a much bigger say on equity prices than what the FOMC actually decided to do. By establishing QE, the Fed effectively created a considerable amount of moral hazard by force-feeding investors risk assets; hence the expression *the foie gras market.*[12]

---

[12] I have borrowed the expression with gratitude from James Montier of GMO.

Exhibit 2.4: S&P 500 performance on days the FOMC meet (%)

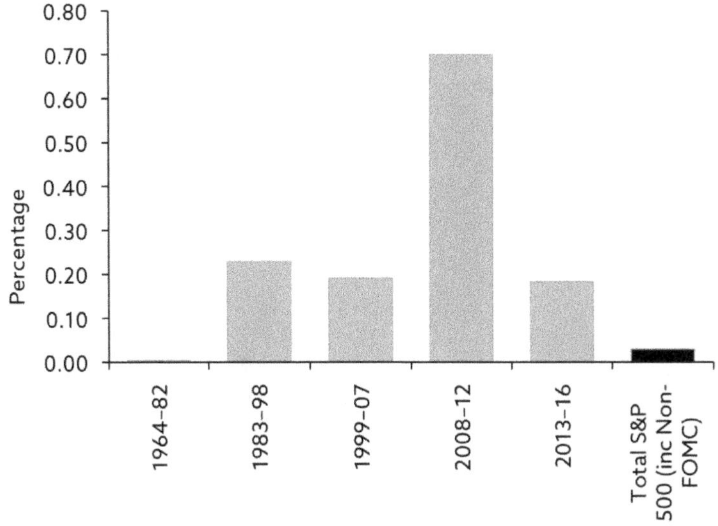

Source: GMO (2016).

The link between monetary policy and financial stability has been discussed repeatedly over the years, but nobody has phrased it more eloquently than the late Nicholas Kaldor when, back in 1958, he wrote:

> "Reliance on monetary policy as an effective stabilising device would involve a high degree of instability. The capital market would become far more speculative [and] profitability would play a subordinate role."

The love affair with the Fed has resulted in very high US CAPE multiples[13] when compared to European CAPE multiples. On the days the FOMC have convened, and only on those days, if one were to replace the actual S&P 500 return with the average daily return, a very different picture would emerge (exhibit 2.5).

---

13   CAPE is a short name for Cyclically Adjusted Price Earnings.

Exhibit 2.5: US policy-adjusted earnings multiple vs. CAPE multiple over time

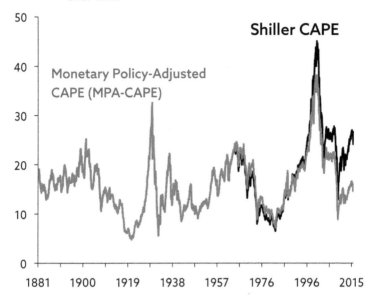

Source: GMO (2016).

As you can see, the CAPE multiple on the S&P 500 would drop from the mid-twenties to the mid-teens, which is much more in line with European CAPE valuations. In other words, if we remove the moral hazard premium created by the Fed, US and European equities are roughly equally expensive (on a CAPE basis). As the love affair with the Fed ends, the multiple spread is therefore likely to narrow; however, nobody knows when that will happen.

That said, we do know, as you will see in chapters 4 and 8, that equity valuations (in theory) should be under much more pressure now than they are, and the reason they are not probably has a lot to do with QE. QE has distorted normal market mechanisms and has kept risk assets at valuation levels that cannot be justified from a fundamental point of view.

It will be very interesting to see what happens to equities and other risk assets when QE is no longer there to support financial markets. Some argue that QE has already been phased out in some countries. Whilst that is technically correct, obese balance sheets in central banks all over the world still offer massive support to risk assets.

Monetary policy's longer-term impact on bonds and equities

As we just saw, average equity returns on those days the FOMC convene have been absurdly high more recently. However, for long-term investors, it is probably more interesting to know how monetary policy affects bond and equity returns in the long run. The Credit Suisse Global Investment Returns Yearbook 2016 looked into that[14].

The authors of the yearbook – Elroy Dimson, Paul Marsh and Mike Staunton – divided past return data into so-called hiking cycles and easing cycles, subject to whether policy rates were either moving up or down during the period[15], and the difference in returns is quite staggering.

During easing cycles, US equities have on average[16] delivered annual returns of 9.3% but only 2.3% during hiking cycles. Meanwhile, US bonds have returned 3.6% annually in easing cycles but only 0.3% annually in hiking cycles. Corresponding data from the UK[17] suggests UK equities also do much better in easing cycles (8.2% vs. 1.7%), whereas UK bonds have generated largely identical returns in the two cycles.

With the Fed having kicked off a new hiking cycle by raising rates in December 2015 for the first time in almost 10 years, one could therefore argue that *regardless* of the structural trends to be discussed later in this

---

14 Source: Elroy Dimson, Paul Marsh and Mike Staunton (2016). All data in this section are from this book.
15 The exact methodology is explained in detail on page 16 of the 2016 yearbook.
16 During the period 1913–2015.
17 Covering the period 1930–2015.

book, we have entered a period, where significant headwinds are to be expected – at least as far as equities are concerned. It is indeed possible that the current hiking cycle dies prematurely, should the Fed (and/or other central banks) move back on recently announced plans, but the structural trends to be reviewed later will not be affected *at all*.

How expensive are equities?

There are many approaches one may take when looking into how expensive equities are. Apart from the fact that valuations may have changed significantly by the time you read this, you also run the risk of comparing apples to oranges.

How do you measure valuation?

Do you focus on price/sales, price/EBITDA (earnings before interest, taxes, depreciation, and amortisation) or price/earnings? Do you prefer to base your calculation on trailing twelve-month (TTM) earnings, forward looking estimates, or do you side with Professor Shiller who prefers the CAPE approach over 10 years? Results may differ quite dramatically subject to which approach you take.

Humans, being the animals we are, often work backwards. We choose the valuation approach that delivers the most convenient result, i.e. we build our case around the valuation parameter that supports our case the best – not the other way around, as we should do.

Even if the CAPE approach is my favourite approach, at present, it matters not a great deal which valuation model I use. Equities are expensive, and US equities are particularly expensive, *regardless* of approach. Consequently, many bulls have resorted to all kinds of creative reasons why valuation doesn't matter anymore. "It's different this time", they say. Apart from it being quite entertaining, it is also a rather hazardous approach.

That said, if one goes back in history, it is indeed possible to find numerous examples of equities being very expensive; yet they have delivered solid, positive returns in subsequent years; i.e. the valuation approach is by no means infallible. However, *on average*, there is indeed a strong link between prevailing valuations and equity market returns the following 10 years, but the link is at best quite weak over shorter periods of time[18].

Going back to exhibit 2.3 for a minute, as you can see, we have had three secular bear markets since World War II. At the end of the first two in 1949 and 1982 respectively, US equities traded at about 6–7 times TTM earnings[19]. However, by the end of the most recent secular bear market in 2009, US P/E multiples had only dropped to about 16 times TTM earnings, which is most likely a function of the substantial damage to corporate earnings caused by the Global Financial Crisis; i.e. equities dropped dramatically, but so did earnings.

An altogether different approach, which I will discuss in chapter 8, is based on total household wealth, and how high wealth is (and should be) as a percentage of GDP. It goes without saying that one cannot outgrow the other forever and, as you will see later, wealth-to-GDP in the US is currently out of sync with past norms – so much that I argue that wealth could drop by as much as 20–25% in the years to come.

At this stage, I shall not go into further detail on this topic; suffice to say that everything points in the same direction. Equities – and particularly US equities – are overvalued. How much they are likely to drop depends on the valuation parameter you tune in on.

Why have equity markets largely ignored fundamentals in recent years?

QE is considered by many the sole reason equities have become so expensive in the years following the Global Financial Crisis but, as we shall see next, it is far from the only reason why equities have rallied, even if it is an important one.

---

[18]   See for example Federal Reserve Bank of Kansas City (2000) or Advisor Perspectives (2017,2).
[19]   Source: Bloomberg.

QE first. As interest rates have plummeted, many investors have resorted to equities. In the first few years following the Global Financial Crisis, many investors also looked to hedge funds to bail them out, but hedge funds have mostly disappointed. The combination of low returns and high fees has been a major turnoff for many.

Consequently, equities have become the only game in town for many investors, driving ever larger pools of capital to this asset class, and that has obviously had an impact on equity valuations. One could therefore – with some right – argue that, as things stand (i.e. with interest rates as low as they are), using past valuation comparisons as your starting point is not necessarily valid when making a call on current valuations.

That said, as interest rates normalise (as they will do eventually), and the appetite for bonds returns, equities will suddenly look outrageously expensive, and the Reckoning Day won't be far away when that happens. The Bank of England (BoE) recognised as much when they, back in 2011, provided the following commentary:

> "The overall effect of asset purchases on the macroeconomy can be broken down into two stages: an initial 'impact' phase and an 'adjustment' phase, during which the stimulus from asset purchases works through the economy [...]. In the impact phase, asset purchases change the composition of the portfolios held by the private sector, increasing holdings of broad money and decreasing those of medium and long-term gilts. But because gilts and broad money are imperfect substitutes, this creates an initial imbalance. As asset portfolios are rebalanced, asset prices are bid up until equilibrium in money and asset markets is restored. This is reinforced by the signalling channel and the other effects of asset purchases already discussed, which may also act to raise asset prices. Through lower borrowing costs and higher wealth, asset prices then raise demand, which acts to push up the consumer price level.
>
> "In the adjustment phase, rising consumer and asset prices raise the demand for money balances and the supply of long-term assets. So the initial imbalance in money and asset markets

shrinks, and *real asset prices begin to fall back* [emphasis mine]. The boost to demand therefore diminishes and the price level continues to increase but by smaller amounts. The whole process continues until the price level has risen sufficiently to restore real money balances, real asset prices and real output to their equilibrium levels. Thus, from a position of deficient demand, asset purchases should accelerate the return of the economy to equilibrium."[20]

In other words, back in 2011, the BoE basically warned investors against excessive exuberance. There will be more difficult times ahead, they said, and they linked that change in fortunes to rising inflation, which they expected to arrive on the back of rising consumer demand.

Why has that not happened?

The flattening of the wage Phillips curve

There is more than one answer to that question, but one factor has played a particularly dominant role. Since the Global Financial Crisis caused havoc, UK corporates have consistently generated more jobs than the BoE expected them to do; yet wage inflation has underperformed expectations. Not only have wages risen less than expected, but significantly so, which has led to a noteworthy flattening of the UK wage Phillips curve (exhibit 2.6),[21] and the picture is largely the same in the US.[22]

---

20   Source: Bank of England (2011).
21   The wage Phillips curve is the relationship between wage inflation and the rate of unemployment.
22   Source: Haldane (2015).

Exhibit 2.6: UK wage Phillips curve over time

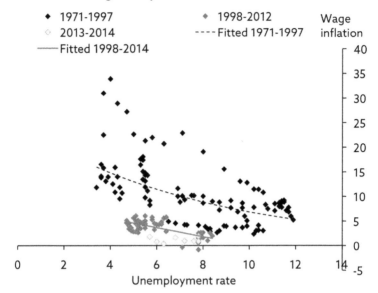

Source: Haldane (2015).

As you can see, more recently, low unemployment has not had nearly the impact on wage inflation it had throughout the 1970s, 1980s and 1990s and, although the Phillips curve already began to flatten in the 2000s, it continues to do so. In part, that reflects weakening productivity growth, which continues to come in below BoE forecasts; however, wage growth has been surprisingly weak, even when adjusting for that.

In chapter 5 I shall discuss this topic in much more detail. Suffice to say for now that the continued flattening of the UK wage Phillips curve is probably linked to labour's shrinking share of national income. As labour has continued to lose out to capital, the growth rate of real wages has turned negative, and living standards have dropped for the median UK household.

Over the decades (and probably centuries), labour and capital have divided national income in a nearly constant fashion. However, in recent decades, that ratio has changed. Capital has taken more and more of national income to the detriment of labour, and it is not only in the UK that this has happened, but more about that in chapter 5.

When will the wage Phillips curve revert to normal?

Should labour begin to capture a rising share of national income, that would probably go a long way to normalise the wage Phillips curve, which is now largely flat in the UK. Taking another look at exhibit 2.6, back in the 1970–90s, once the unemployment rate dropped below 6–7%, it was quite normal for wage inflation to accelerate beyond 10%. Not anymore. Regardless of what the unemployment rate has been more recently, UK wage inflation has been nearly non-existent.

Could that be related to the growing automation of industry?

Are people so afraid of losing their jobs to robots that they ask for little or no pay rises? Although it is hard to prove, at least in my mind, there can be no doubt that this is a factor to be reckoned with. Over the decades, few jobs have been lost as a consequence of better and more sophisticated technology. What has instead happened is that the workforce has up-skilled. However, the fear factor is what drives behaviour, not facts, and many workers are fearful of losing out to robots.

I have found virtually no correlation between the use of robots and employment in the manufacturing industry. Robots don't cost jobs (at least not on a grand scale) – poor competitiveness does. Brexit will lead to improved competitiveness and hence more jobs, many Brexiters argue, but I would suggest you take a sneak preview of exhibit 10.2, which depicts the penetration of advanced robotics around the world. Brexit is not at all the answer to Britain's poor competitiveness. Low penetration of advanced robotics is.

The key driver of advanced robotics – the cost advantage

The market for advanced robotics is in reality four different markets – personal, commercial, industrial and military. The industrial segment is the largest, but the personal segment is expected to grow the fastest.

The industry that has been penetrated the most by robots so far is the automotive industry, and it is not difficult to understand why. A spot-welder working in the US automotive industry is paid about three times as much as a spot-welding robot can do the job for (all in)[23], and the difference will only get bigger in the years to come.

The world will change dramatically as a result of advanced robotics, but is it for the better or worse? I have come across estimates suggesting that robots will take over nearly 50% of all manufacturing jobs and shave $9 trillion off labour costs within a decade[24]. Whether these numbers are accurate, only time can tell, but the trend is clear, and the driver is first mover advantage. Those countries that don't embrace the new technology will simply be left behind, such are the advantages, but more on this in chapter 10.

The impact on inflation – the two extremes

Let's revisit BofAML's projection that 50% of all manufacturing jobs will be lost between now and 2025. That could potentially raise unemployment levels quite dramatically and, by implication, increase the economic slack, which would almost certainly put further downward pressure on inflation.

As far as labour market projections are concerned, the two extreme cases in the Western world are the US and Germany[25]. Whereas the US

---

23   Source: BofAML (2015).
24   Source: BofAML (2015).
25   I have chosen to conveniently ignore the fact that, in some respects, both the Japanese and the Italian outlooks are even more dire than the German.

workforce will continue to grow (modestly), the German workforce will shrink substantially between now and 2050[26].

In the US, 15.4 million people are employed in manufacturing[27]. Consequently, if BofAML is about right, 7.7 million workers should lose their jobs over the next 10 years. That's a shade under 5% of the US workforce.

On top of that, according to United Nations data, the US workforce should grow by about 0.25% annually between now and 2050. Consequently, it may prove more difficult than it normally would for new job market entrants to land their first job.

Now, compare those stats to those of Germany. In Germany, 7.9 million workers are employed in manufacturing, so 3.95 million are at risk of losing their jobs if BofAML projections are correct but, because of ageing, the German workforce will, unlike the US workforce, shrink considerably in the years to come.

The German civilian workforce is made up of 42 million people[28] but, according to UN data, it is expected to shrink by 0.8% annually between now and 2050. In other words, by 2050, the German workforce should be down to about 31.7 million workers – a drop of more than 10 million workers between now and 2050.

Although the fall is back-end loaded (most will drop out of the workforce between 2030 and 2050), for the case of simplicity, let's assume it is a straight line, which would imply that the German workforce will have fallen by 3¼ million people by 2025 – 10 years after BofAML made their projection that almost 4 million Germans are at risk of losing their jobs to robots between 2015 and 2025.

The conclusion is straightforward. Whereas automation could put severe pressure on the US manufacturing workforce, a shrinking German workforce (caused by ageing) will effectively deal with that challenge.

---

[26]   This will be discussed in much more detail in chapter 4.
[27]   Source: OECD.
[28]   Source: OECD.

The outlook for the UK

The UK outlook is somewhere between those two extremes. The UK civilian workforce was 32.6 million people in 2015 and is estimated to grow by 0.1% annually between now and 2050, implying that the UK workforce should have grown by 1.2 million workers by then.

Now, if you remember my point from a little earlier, you will recall that the UK doesn't do particularly well in the automation league tables. One could argue that, with a (modestly) growing workforce, the UK doesn't face the same need to automate that Germany does, and that is indeed correct if the sole purpose is to keep manufacturing jobs alive. However, if the British want to compete internationally, they don't really have a choice but to ramp up automation.

Investment implications

As we already know, equities have not exactly done poorly since the Global Financial Crisis; nor are they priced particularly attractively at current levels. Other things being equal, this would leave them rather exposed to any sort of adverse developments.

This book is not exactly short of adverse developments about to unfold, but much more about that in the next seven chapters. For now, I will keep it simple. Equities have entered a policy rate hiking cycle, suggesting substantial headwinds in the years to come. Simply put, in the foreseeable future, equities will *not* deliver the sorts of returns they have delivered since 1982.

Be prepared for much more modest returns, but don't necessarily expect the picture to be uniform across the world. As we have just seen, certain dynamics will affect certain countries far more than others. For example, ageing is a much bigger issue in Europe than it is in the US, but that is not entirely negative.

Rapid ageing of the German populace will indeed have a significant (and negative) impact on economic growth in that country but, as we just saw, the introduction of advanced robotics could potentially be the solution to Germany's ageing problem, as it will allow German industry to continue as if nothing has happened. Meanwhile, in the US, a growing workforce will force those in power to choose between full employment and being able to compete internationally.

One can therefore not assume that financial markets across the world will react uniformly to a rising degree of automation. Significant interest rate gaps could open up, and equity market returns could vary quite dramatically, but more on that in chapter 12.

3

The End of the Debt Super-Cycle

Is debt good or bad for economic growth? Few topics divide the investment community more than this question. Most investors would probably agree that some debt is good for economic growth, but there is no strong consensus as to how much debt is good, and when it turns counter-productive. In this chapter, I will look at debt in a historical perspective, and why we are approaching the end of the current debt super-cycle.

The nature of debt super-cycles

IN A DEBT super-cycle, as the cycle advances, economic growth is increasingly driven by a combination of growth in debt and money supply. Having said that, there are obviously limits as to how much spending can be financed by debt and money. When that point is reached, you are at the end of the debt super-cycle. John Maynard Keynes called it Push on a String, when he first described the phenomenon in 1935. Nowadays, it is often called the Liquidity Trap.

When debt rises fast – and fast in this context means faster than GDP growth – capital that could otherwise be used productively to enhance GDP growth is instead used to service existing debt, i.e. it is used unproductively.

Debt rising faster than GDP is a vicious circle. As GDP growth slows, more debt is needed to service existing debt, which will cause GDP growth to slow even further. Debt therefore continues to grow, and GDP growth continues to slow, until it all ends in tears.

What we are now beginning to see are the first signs of Push on a String. When that happens, monetary policy is already so accommodative that further rate cuts have virtually no effect on economic growth. QE also becomes largely ineffective, as risk premia are too low to drive investors to assume more risk. The very low returns that we currently see across almost all asset classes is a classic sign that we are approaching the end of the debt super-cycle.

How much longer can the current debt super-cycle last for?

Overall debt levels have been rising in most countries pretty much without interruption since the end of World War II and, for that reason, the debt super-cycle we are currently in is widely perceived to be about 70 years old. Debt super-cycles, which have existed for centuries, last 50+ years on average[29], so it is no wonder that many investors are getting a bit worried.

Debt levels do appear to be rather elevated at present. Debt-to-GDP in mature economies continues to rise incessantly, and emerging markets are slowly catching up. Before the Global Financial Crisis, financial leverage in emerging markets was a relatively modest 146% of GDP, but it is now well over 200% (exhibit 3.1).

The Global Financial Crisis was largely caused by excessive levels of debt, and one would therefore assume that many had learned an important lesson, but far from it. Since 2006 – the last year before the Global Financial Crisis took control – global debt has increased by about $72 trillion, dramatically outpacing global GDP growth. Even more

---

[29]   Source: Ray Dalio, Bridgewater Associates (2016).

noticeable, not a single OECD country has de-levered since 2007, and only a handful of emerging market countries have managed to do so.

Exhibit 3.1: Total global debt, USD (all sectors, % of GDP)

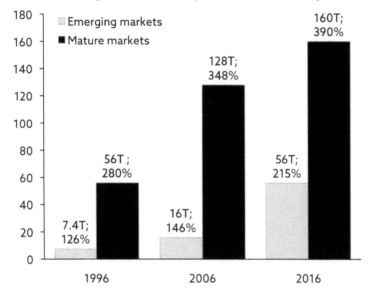

Source: Institute of International Finance (2017).

The post-crisis increase in debt varies a great deal from sector to sector. The financial sector is the only one of the four main sectors that have managed to de-lever to any meaningful degree since the financial crisis.

Leverage in the non-financial corporate sector remains at a very high level but has hardly changed in recent years, whereas the household sector has de-levered modestly, but not nearly as much as the financial sector. The public sector, meanwhile, has taken the skunk prize. Enormous amounts of additional debt have been established, and the sector is solely responsible for the overall rise in financial leverage since 2008[30] (exhibit 3.2).

---

30   Much of the increase in government debt since the Global Financial Crisis has been caused by governments bailing out various financial institutions.

Exhibit 3.2: Total debt by sector in mature economies

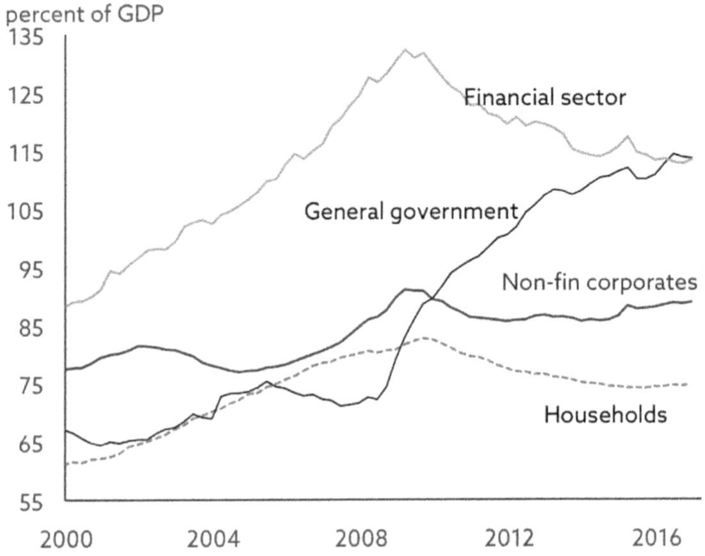

percent of GDP

Source: Institute of International Finance (2017).

This raises the question – how much longer can this possibly go on for?

There is no doubt that the extraordinarily low interest rate environment much of the world has enjoyed in recent years is a significant part of the reason behind the continued appetite for debt, but what would happen if interest rates were to normalise?

Have borrowers become debt junkies just because it is so cheap to borrow these days?

Before I answer those questions, allow me to make a few comments on debt vis-à-vis QE, which is often blamed for the continued rise in debt levels post 2008. Total debt levels have certainly been impacted by QE, but you should note that overall debt levels began to rise decades ago, long before anyone had ever heard of QE.

The previous debt super-cycle ended with the Great Depression in the 1930s and World War II. As the war came to an end, the world was in need of major re-construction following six years of devastation, and a new debt super-cycle was formed – the one we are now at the tail-end of.

Debt accumulation in the post-crisis environment

Let's re-visit exhibit 3.1 for a moment. When looking at the numbers, it is obvious that debt continues to grow almost as if 2008 never happened. Going into the Global Financial Crisis, total worldwide debt stood at $144 trillion, up a rather dramatic $80 trillion from 1996. Rapidly rising debt was considered the main culprit behind the Global Financial Crisis[31], and one would expect both debtors and creditors to have learned a very serious lesson.

However, by 2016, global debt had risen to $216 trillion, dramatically outpacing global GDP growth. As GDP growth slowed, more debt needed to be established to service existing debt which, at least so far, has caused GDP growth to slow even further. Debt will continue to rise and GDP growth will continue to slow, until we hit the proverbial wall, which marks the end of the debt super-cycle.

What happens in the later stages of debt super-cycles is in effect a gigantic misallocation of capital. How significant it is, is best illustrated by looking at the velocity of money in the US, which is now at the lowest level of the last 70 years (exhibit 3.3).

---

[31] If you have a desire to learn more about the reasons for the Global Financial Crisis, I would encourage you to read Mervyn King's account of it, as he offers a somewhat more complex explanation for the crisis. He distinguishes between the Good (a period of unprecedented stability of both output and inflation), the Bad (the rise in debt levels) and the Ugly (the development of an extremely fragile banking system). The crisis, he says, was the result of the Good, the Bad and the Ugly failing at the same time. See Mervyn King (2016).

Exhibit 3.3: US velocity of money (M2)

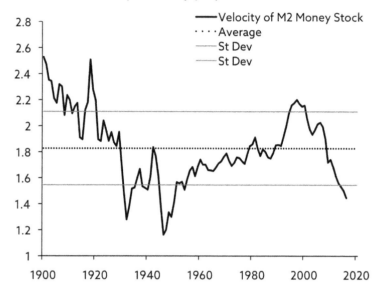

Source: Bawerk (2017)

Velocity of US money is now down to levels last seen towards the end of the last debt super-cycle. Velocity of money is calculated as total output (GDP) divided by total money supply (in this case M2). When the velocity of money drops, GDP isn't growing at the same pace as money supply.

QE has led to a significant rise in money supply, and low interest rates have resulted in a massive misallocation of capital (for the reasons mentioned earlier), which has caused the economy to grow at such an abysmal rate. Many inefficient corporates, that should never have had access to capital in the first place, have taken advantage of the combination of relatively easy access to capital and low borrowing costs.

The link between the credit cycle and GDP growth

I am often confronted with the question: if debt is so good for economic growth, why on earth is GDP growth so weak at present?

Back in 2008, Michael Biggs, an economist at Deutsche Bank, introduced the concept of Credit Impulse, which he defined as the change in new credit issued as a % of GDP. He found a very powerful link between that and private sector demand, and that explains the conundrum above. The critics typically focus on the credit stock, whereas Biggs focused on credit flows.

If you go back to your school days and dig out the definition of GDP, you may recall that:

$$GDP = C + I + G + (X - M)$$

where C denotes consumer spending, I is a measure of investments, G is public spending, and X − M represent net exports. Consequently, C+I is a proxy for private sector demand, and Michael Biggs found that the Credit Impulse is almost perfectly correlated with C+I.

It is therefore only reasonable to assume that GDP growth also correlates quite highly with the Credit Impulse, i.e. the growth in credit. Consequently, it seems fair to conclude that those who argue that debt is *never* good, are plainly wrong. Yet, they frequently refer to the paltry GDP growth rate in recent years to prove their point.

My point is a different one. The Global Financial Crisis was caused by abnormally high debt levels in certain sectors and countries, and monetary authorities responded by lowering interest rates – both at the near-end (through policy rates) and the long-end (through QE). To begin with, such a strategy made sense, but it is way past its sell-by date now. We have reached a point where the solution (low interest rates) is causing more damage than the problem itself (high debt levels).

Low interest rates lead to lower productivity growth

Low interest rates damage economic growth through the negative impact they have on productivity. The logic is as follows. The fall in interest rates ever since the early 1980s has led to a monumental bull market in credit and equity markets, lasting over 30 years. Consequently, the financial sector has grown dramatically almost everywhere.

The financial sector competes with the rest of the economy for resources (human as well as capital), and strong growth in the relatively well-paid financial sector has drained other sectors of resources, which has impacted productivity negatively[32]. It effectively backs up my conclusion from earlier, i.e. that low interest rates lead to an increase in misallocated capital, which again leads to lower productivity growth.

Furthermore, low interest rates keep inefficient companies alive (more misallocated capital), particularly when access to capital is relatively easy, and that has indeed been the case in the US in recent years, and is increasingly the case in the UK. Many inefficient corporates are kept artificially alive by low rates. A zombie economy has been established.

Another drag on economic growth is excess growth in credit. This is because credit booms harm the more R&D-intensive engines of economic growth. This is a poorly understood side effect of low interest rates combined with strong credit growth, and is becoming a real issue for some countries, particularly the Anglo-Saxon ones, where the financial sector is much bigger than in most other countries.

Low interest rates lead to more risk taking

Investors not only take on more debt when the debt service burden is low; they also take more risk, potentially leading to further asset bubbles. Since 2008, investors have distinguished less between different types of risk. They have either been in 'risk on' or 'risk off' mode.

---

32   Source: BIS (2015,2).

Then again, due to the extraordinarily lenient behaviour of most central banks more recently, investors in general, and US investors in particular, have managed to convince themselves that central banks will do whatever is necessary to prevent the ship from sinking.

At least twice in recent years, equity investors have chosen to ignore indicators pointing towards an economic slowdown, and that is most likely due to an almost limitless belief in the put option provided by central banks. In early 2013, the Fed launched QE3 in the US and, in early 2015, the ECB launched QE1 in the Eurozone. In both instances, global equities chose to ignore a deteriorating economic cycle. Risk-on, risk-off miraculously turned into risk-on, risk-on. "Don't fight the Fed", as they say, and equity investors obviously chose not to.

Low interest rates equal major problems for DB pension schemes

Those corporates whose liabilities are effectively a function of interest rates have experienced by far the biggest problems in recent years. Take defined benefit (DB) pension schemes, of which there are many around the world, although some countries are far more exposed to DB schemes than others (exhibit 3.4).

DB schemes calculate the present value of future liabilities by discounting the entitlements they must pay out to their members in the years to come, using the yield on longer-dated bonds[33]. If bond yields fall, pension funds are forced to use a lower discount rate, and that increases the present value of future liabilities.

Those liabilities will also rise if their members live longer than planned. In both instances, the pension scheme's funded status deteriorates, which is why so many DB pension schemes around the world have significant funding problems at present. Their liabilities are meaningfully higher than the value of their assets.

---

[33] Which types of bonds differ from country to country and from DB scheme to DB scheme.

Exhibit 3.4: Total assets in occupational DB and DC schemes, 2015 (USD million)[34]

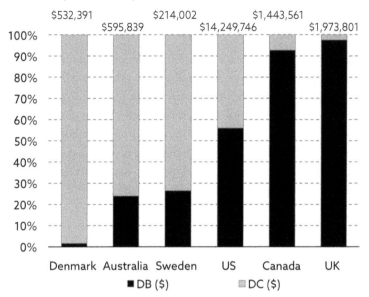

Source: OECD (2016).

It all adds up to the perfect storm. Risk assets don't do well enough to keep up with the rise in liabilities, and falling interest rates cause those liabilities to grow even faster. Adding to that, members live longer and longer.

The result?

My guess is a dramatic overhaul of the entire pension system in the years to come. Otherwise we are likely to see some quite spectacular blow-ups.

---

34   Excluding personal pension plans, which in some countries account for a very significant percentage of total pension savings. In the US, for example, assets under management in IRAs account for more than 1/3 of total pension assets under management, and personal pension plans are DC in nature.

The financial regulator in Denmark saw the writing on the wall years ago and forced Danish pension funds to hedge their interest rate risk. In turn, Danish pension funds managed to convert most of their members to DC schemes, where the risks are effectively transferred from the employer to the employees.

That has had two major effects. Firstly, there are few unfunded pension liabilities in the Danish system today and, secondly, because pension funds are no longer subject to the same restrictions in terms of what they can invest in, most Danish pension funds have since delivered much better returns to their members than peers in countries dominated by DB schemes. I think the rest of the world will eventually follow the Danish model.

The UK pension industry has done little to that effect, and the problems are there for everybody to see. According to the latest official estimate (from 2012), total pension liabilities are just over £7 trillion, £4.8 trillion of which are unfunded. Industry sources tell me that, as of late 2017, unfunded pension liabilities in the UK are about £11 trillion – more than five times UK GDP.

Put another way, £11 trillion translate into approximately £400,000 per UK household in unfunded pension liabilities; a whopping number that makes pretty much all other problems look like a walk in the park. The fact that most of those unfunded pension liabilities in the UK represent state liabilities only makes matters worse. There is only one place to find the money – the taxpayer's pockets.

Some countries have begun to act. Take the US, where the regulator now allows the industry to use the average yield over the last 25 years when discounting future liabilities back to a present value. Although that has had the effect of reducing the present value of future liabilities and thus the amount of unfunded liabilities, it does absolutely nothing in terms of addressing the core of the problem. It is akin to offering a plaster to a patient, who needs major surgery.

And things get worse. The liability challenge is not only a problem facing the pension industry. It is indeed a challenge for any firm whose liabilities are at least partially a function of the prevailing yield on bonds. I have chosen not to go into any level of detail on this aspect, but many companies in the financial industry (e.g. life insurers) could be in major trouble, if interest rates don't rise relatively soon.

The end of the debt super-cycle – what happens next?

What will happen once the debt super-cycle is well and truly over? Nobody knows, as there are more than half a million different possible outcomes, but some are more likely than others. The last debt super-cycle ended with the Great Depression and World War II, the latter of which started the present debt super-cycle, as the world woke up to a great need of reconstruction in 1945.

That said, don't expect me to get into the business of making silly forecasts like those two. I see one of the following five outcomes (and possibly a combination) as the most likely end to the current debt super-cycle:

1. Delay and pray

My opening forecast, and the one I assign the highest probability to, is that policy makers will hope they can muddle through by keeping interest rates at comparatively low levels for many years to come, and that means at least until the mid-2020s (more on the implications of *delay and pray* in chapter 11). There are admittedly some noticeable differences from country to country – particularly as far as demographics are concerned.

For example, ageing of the populace is a much bigger issue in Europe than it is in the US, and for that reason economic growth in Europe will likely be negatively impacted as far out as 2050, but I will go into much more detail on that issue in chapter 4. Suffice to say for now that I don't expect dramatically higher interest rates anywhere in the developed world for at least another six to eight years.

In a credit context, the most important reason interest rates are likely to stay low for quite a while is that, as you approach the proverbial wall I referred to earlier, the debt super-cycle turns into a de facto de-leveraging cycle, and de-leveraging always takes longer to complete than you think at the outset.

You don't necessarily spot the overall desire to de-lever at first glance, as total debt continues to rise, but the debt composition between sectors changes. Governments, keen to avoid a systemic meltdown, step in and bail out private sector debtors, who are keen to de-lever.

2. One or more sovereign defaults

As a natural consequence of this, I would expect public sector debt to continue to grow for quite a while yet, and I would also expect some sovereign defaults in the developed world before this is all over. Sovereign defaults can take many different forms and, in today's environment, I don't think we are likely to see a simple and straightforward default from any advanced economy. The implications are quite simply too dramatic for that to happen.

However, as I said, sovereigns can default in many ways. Take the UK government's exposure to pension entitlements that I discussed earlier in this chapter. Raising the retirement age to 70 would go a long way to address the funding deficit but, technically, it is a default, as the government no longer honours prior commitments.

I would go one step further and suggest that one of the more likely outcomes of the end of the debt super-cycle is a collapse of the entire pension system as we know it today, and for it to be completely revamped – and that would most likely include a total stop to DB schemes.

This process has already started in many countries, but the conversion from DB to DC has either been voluntary so far, or it has only comprised new members and/or new schemes. I suspect the conversion at some point will become mandatory for existing members as well. That's how big the problem is (in some countries).

3. Austerity

The gentleman's version of sovereign default is austerity which is not, as the Greeks learned a few years ago, immensely popular amongst ordinary people. However, austerity is what happens when you don't follow the rules, but desperately try to avoid bankruptcy.

The problem facing society today is that we have a large and very influential generation that happens to be in power – the baby boom generation. Baby boomers have been brought up in a climate of uninterrupted economic progress, and they clearly don't always understand the meaning of the word *no*. That said, as governments start to deal with the tail-end of the debt super-cycle, baby boomers will learn how to spell austerity, even in Swahili.

4. Government budgeting

Another outcome that I expect from the current debt super-cycle is that governments will increasingly distinguish between fiscal deficits caused by transfer payments and deficits caused by growth-enhancing investment projects; in other words, governments will start to provide not one but two budgets.

After all, investors will be much more willing to finance deficits caused by productivity-enhancing infrastructure projects, as long as spending on transfer payments is fully funded by tax payers. That this is not just wishful thinking on my behalf was confirmed to me in recent discussions I had with government officials in both Washington and London. It was confirmed to me that there are indeed discussions along those lines in both countries.

5. A regulatory overhaul

Furthermore, I would expect a complete – and rather dramatic – overhaul of the banking industry, serving the purpose of making society less dependent on banks' wellbeing. Going forward, banks will primarily service tier one corporate clients. Small and medium-sized companies, and to some degree also retail customers, will increasingly go elsewhere with their banking business.

The problem in a nutshell is that the balance sheets of most banks, after years of rapid growth, have simply grown too big, and regulatory authorities are now keen to drive the leverage in the financial sector down to more reasonable levels again. As I prepared for this book, it became evident to me that US banks are more open for business than European banks are at present, but tier two and tier three corporates are not finding it easy anywhere.

Not that long ago, a senior official of a major European bank told me that European banks are under tremendous regulatory pressure to reduce the size of their loan books. Total bank loans in Europe add up to about €18 trillion, he said[35], whereas the equivalent number in the US is only $8 trillion, and the two economies are not miles apart size-wise. If the regulatory authorities succeed with the downsizing of the European banking industry, economic growth could suffer quite meaningfully.

Investment implications

And now a few thoughts on portfolio construction in a post-debt super-cycle environment.

My investment advice, first and foremost, is not to venture too far out on the risk curve. You only do that in raving bull markets, and we are not in one at present.

Corporate debt below investment grade is quite a fashionable item these days, but the asset class will almost certainly take a knock when we hit the proverbial wall. Investment grade bonds, on the other hand, could do surprisingly well. The mother of all bear markets in bonds, as predicted by some, is very unlikely to unfold for many years to come, if my vision proves correct.

---

35   Using the European Banking Federation as his source.

Equities are a little different. Debt super-cycles rarely end without significant damage to equities, and I would be very surprised if this one is going to be fundamentally different. There is one significant difference, though, when I compare the current cycle to past debt super-cycles.

Large institutional investors such as pension funds didn't exist in prior debt super-cycles. Many of those investors *must* invest regardless, and they account for a substantial chunk of overall demand for equities. Consequently, the impact on equities may not be quite as dramatic as predicted by some of the more pessimistic forecasters in the financial industry.

In the equity space I favour income-generating equities, but I would disregard those companies that pay attractive dividends without generating the required cash flow internally. A surprisingly large number of companies borrow to pay attractive dividends, and they will struggle in a post-debt super-cycle environment.

My second advice is to zoom in on alternative investment opportunities. The world, as we know it, is likely to be very different in a post-debt super-cycle environment. One of the most dramatic changes is likely to be the role of the banking industry. As mentioned earlier, apart from tier one corporates, much of what we have taken for granted in the past will be no more.

From an investment point of view, that has opened a very interesting door. Alternative lenders (alternative to commercial banks) are popping up left, right and centre, and most of them operate at a fraction of the cost of commercial banks. Their knowledge and expertise is often intact, though, as many alternative lending teams are simply breakout teams from commercial banks.

Adding to that, due to the limited competition from traditional lenders, margins are relatively good, at least for now, but that may obviously change. If banking regulators become more accommodating, commercial banks will be breathing down the necks of their new competitors, and margins will drop like a stone.

Furthermore, as the need for income in an ageing world is significantly higher than the amount of investment opportunities in the alternative lending space, too much capital continues to flow into the space, driving down expected returns.

Most importantly, though, it is my experience that there are quite a few opportunists operating in the alternative lending space. That is a *massive* risk to take for the uninitiated. Opportunists rarely do their homework properly, but they are usually very good marketing people, which tends to win most investors over. All I can say is: do your homework properly or pay somebody to do it for you. This investment strategy is not as simple as it sounds.

Thirdly, I would add gold to my portfolio. In over 30 years in the financial industry, I have *never* recommended adding physical gold to anyone's portfolio, but gold is the ultimate currency in a world of extreme uncertainty, and the end of the debt super-cycle is likely to cause a great deal of uncertainty, hence my advice.

You have probably figured this out already, but I am certainly not a gold buff – far from it. I have always seen gold primarily as a hedge against inflation but, as I prepared for this book I changed my mind as I came to realise that gold is a hedge against uncertainty more so than against inflation.

The more wheels that come off as the world de-levers, the more likely it is for the financial industry to sustain some serious damage and, when that happens, you never know what could happen next. Consequently, I would recommend the most conservative investors to buy gold bullion and store it somewhere safe, but to all those (and I am in that camp myself) who believe that the financial industry will survive as we know it today, buying synthetic gold (e.g. an ETF on gold) is most likely good enough. It certainly is for me.

4

The Retirement of the Baby Boomers

Older consumers spend less money overall, and they spend their money quite differently when compared to younger consumers. It is therefore only reasonable to expect an ageing population to have a profound impact on economic growth and financial markets for many years to come. There is more to the story than that, though. How do the elderly spend their money? Could ageing possibly be inflationary? These and other questions will be addressed in the following chapter.

The retiring boomers

As World War II came to an end, people all over the western world regained the appetite for having children, and millions of them were born in an extraordinary bull market for children that lasted almost 20 years. A generation was born that we would come to know as the *baby boom generation.*

Baby boomers have had a positive impact on economic growth and financial markets for a long time. The workforce grew exceptionally fast from the early 1960s to the mid-1970s, as many boomers moved into adulthood. More importantly, in the 1980s and 1990s, as most boomers turned middle-aged and moved into their peak spending years, the foundation of the Great Bull Market was established.

Now, as the oldest boomers have turned 70, they have begun to retire in substantial numbers and, over the next many years, millions of them will do so. In other words, what has been one of the most important reasons behind the extraordinarily good times we have enjoyed since the early 1980s, will almost certainly turn into a headwind for many years to come.

Rob Arnott and his team at Research Affiliates have done some of the most interesting work in the field of demographics. In a paper from 2013[36] they made a very valid point:

> "If we expect our policy elite to deliver implausible growth, in an environment in which a demographic tailwind has become a demographic headwind, they will deliver temporary outsized 'growth' with debt-financed consumption (deficit spending). If we resist the necessary policy changes that can moderate these headwinds, we risk magnifying their impact."

Countries will be impacted differently, though. The United States, having a larger group of echo boomers[37] than most other countries, is likely to see GDP growth re-accelerate sometime in the mid-2020s, whereas many other countries will see demographics having a negative impact on GDP growth for decades to come (exhibit 4.1).

---

36 Source: Research Affiliates (2013).
37 Children of the baby boomers are often called echo boomers.

Exhibit 4.1: Long-term working-age population projections

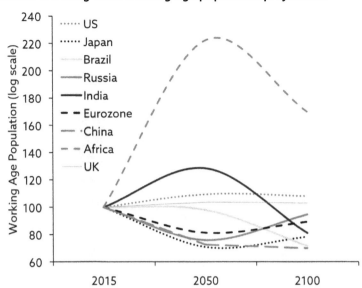

Source: United Nations (2015).

Note 1: Eurozone comprises: France, Germany, Italy and Spain.

Note 2: Africa comprises: Nigeria, Ethiopia, Egypt, Dem. Republic of the Congo, South Africa, Tanzania, Kenya, Sudan, Algeria, Uganda, Morocco, Mozambique, Ghana, Angola and Ivory Coast.

The rapid ageing of the world

The world is ageing at a rapid pace. Between now and 2050, the number of people aged 60 and over will almost double as a share of the total number of people, and the 80+ age group will grow even faster. By the turn of the next century, the 80+ age group will account for almost as big a share of global population as the 60+ age group does today (exhibit 4.2).

Exhibit 4.2: Number of people aged 60 or over (globally, % of total)

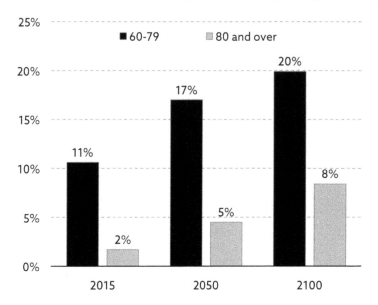

Source: United Nations (2016).

For the first time the old will outnumber the young and, contrary to popular thinking, it is not a phenomenon only to be found in mature economies. Two-thirds of the world's elderly live in emerging market countries, and the number of people aged 65 and over in those countries will rise from 387 million in 2015 to no less than 1,218 million by 2050[38].

China is a noticeable example. Its old-age dependency ratio[39] was 12% in 2010, and by 2050 it is expected to reach 39%. Only a handful of countries around the world will have more old people when measured as a percentage of the overall population.

---

38   Source: United Nations (2015).

39   The old-age dependency ratio is defined as the ratio between the number of people aged 65 and over (deemed the retirees) and the number of people between the age of 15 and 64 (deemed to be a proxy for the workforce). In other words, you measure how many there are in the workforce to pay for the elderly.

In the context of how quickly most countries age, I also find it noteworthy that it took France over 150 years for the average age of its population to double. By comparison, it has taken countries like China and Thailand only about 20.

Ageing will affect us all. Older people not only spend less money than the young do, they also spend it differently. Hence it is not unrealistic to expect ageing to have a significant bearing on economic growth, but it doesn't stop there. Inflation is also likely to be impacted, although there is widespread disagreement as to exactly *how* ageing affects inflation (more about this later).

And because older people spend their money differently, there will also be winners; companies and entire industries that will do much better as people age, even if overall GDP growth slows.

Some country-specific challenges

Deteriorating demographics represent the single most important structural trend that mankind is faced with today, and it will have a massive impact on economic growth, interest rates, public debt, equity markets, etc. As I pointed out in chapter 3, one of the most important repercussions is the effect it will have on our pension systems.

As you may recall, in the UK, unfunded pension liabilities[40] are approximately £11 trillion[41]. By comparison, UK GDP is about £2 trillion. In other words, unfunded UK pension liabilities are now 5–6 times the country's annual output. Younger people had better get used to the fact that they won't receive the pension entitlements they have been promised. The government simply cannot afford to pay out, but nobody wants to start the debate, as it is most certainly not a vote winner.

---

[40]   Unfunded UK pension liabilities have been calculated as the sum of unfunded corporate liabilities, unfunded liabilities at local authorities and state pensions which are, by definition, unfunded.

[41]   According to my source (a senior UK pension consultant), even if the government won't admit it.

Germany is another country with major challenges ahead of it. Germany suffers from having a very high number of elderly when compared to most other countries, but many investors have expressed the view to me that one shouldn't really worry about it until 2030. It is indeed correct that the problem peaks between 2030 and 2050, but it would be a terrible mistake to ignore the problem for another 10 years or so.

The German old-age dependency ratio will rise from just under 36% in 2020 to over 47% in 2030[42]. This implies that, whereas they have approximately three working-aged adults to pay for each elderly in Germany today, they will only have two by 2030. Such a drastic increase in the number of elderly will have a profound effect on German society and, as I said, it is only the starter. The main course will be served between 2030 and 2050!

Finally, a word on Japan: I note that the old-age dependency ratio in the world's oldest country, Japan, reached 35% in 2010, and the number is expected to more than double to 74% by 2050. By comparison, the global average was 12% in 2010, and is expected to reach 25% by 2050[43]. Given the Japanese numbers, one may wonder how much a country can actually cope with. After all, there needs be somebody left to pay the bills.

Nobody knows the answer to that question, as no country has *ever* been in this position before, but I don't think it is a coincidence that Japan is playing games with helicopter money. After all, not that many years from now, they may have no other option.

Ageing's impact on economic growth

Ageing's impact on economic growth is measured in different ways. Some consider the dependency ratio the most appropriate measure, whereas others zoom in on the old-age dependency ratio. My own preferred measure of ageing's impact on economic growth is slightly

---

42   Source: Eurostat (2016).
43   Source: The Economist (2009).

different. I almost always use the percentage change in the absolute size of the workforce, but the difference between the various measures is subtle.

In short, the dependency ratio is a measure that shows the number of dependents – those younger than 15 plus those aged 65 and over – to the total number of people deemed of working age (those aged between 15 and 64). This ratio is sometimes referred to as the total dependency ratio. A variation of this measure is the old-age dependency ratio, where you only measure those aged 65 and over to the working age group.

As mentioned earlier, when forecasting GDP growth, I prefer to work with the percentage change in the absolute size of the workforce, though. That number can be used directly when forecasting the impact of ageing on economic growth. You may recall the following equation from chapter 1:

$$\Delta GDP = \Delta Workforce + \Delta Productivity$$

However, that is an adaption of the following economic identity:

$$\Delta Output = \Delta Number\ of\ hours\ worked + \Delta Output\ per\ hour$$

Output equals GDP, and output per hour is a synonym for productivity. The only tricky part is the change in the number of hours worked. It is not easily tracked but, fortunately, there is a solution. In most countries, the size of the workforce is tracked very closely and, almost everywhere, the workforce puts in largely the same number of hours from one year to the next, allowing us to use changes in the workforce as a proxy for the variation in the number of hours worked. Hence the two equations above are virtually identical.

Consequently, provided you know how much the workforce will grow (or shrink) in the years to come, it is possible to make quite accurate estimates as to the expected long-term change in GDP growth. This is possible because productivity, when viewed over the longer term, rarely changes much.

Obviously, cyclicality introduces some unpredictability in the short term, as productivity may be meaningfully affected by economic swing factors, so the method only works well over at least one full economic cycle. I never use this approach to estimate GDP growth from one year to the next, but it is a very good indicator of trend growth.

As far as the workforce is concerned, given certain assumptions[44], we know almost exactly how much it is going to change in the years to come, we have that information by country, and it doesn't make for very enjoyable reading. In the OECD, the country that will be hit the hardest by a shrinking workforce is not surprisingly Japan, which will see its workforce decline by about 1% annually between now and 2050 (exhibit 4.3).

A fall of that magnitude implies that, if productivity doesn't increase by at least 1% annually in Japan between now and 2050, the country will suffer from negative GDP growth between now and then. Cyclicality will ensure that individual years could end up being significantly different, whether better or worse, but the implication is clear. A shrinking workforce will make it extraordinarily difficult for some countries to post decent GDP growth for many years to come.

As you can also see from exhibit 4.3, of the major developed economies, the country to be least affected by ageing is the United States. Annual workforce growth of about 0.25% will ensure that the US will almost certainly continue to be the fastest growing OECD country for many years to come.

The workforce in the Eurozone will shrink by 0.57% annually, primarily driven by a sharp decline in two of its largest member states, Germany and Italy. The EU workforce (ex. the UK) will decline by no less than 0.64% annually between now and 2050. Had the UK decided to stay in the EU, the annual EU decline would drop from -0.64% to -0.54%. In

---

44　We don't know the exact size of the global workforce, as the retirement age varies from country to country, but we have reliable data on the projected growth on those aged 15–59 (from the United Nations (2015)), which is an excellent proxy for the entire workforce.

other words, the loss of the UK will cost the EU 0.1% in annual GDP growth between now and 2050.

Exhibit 4.3: Estimated annual workforce growth in selected countries and regions

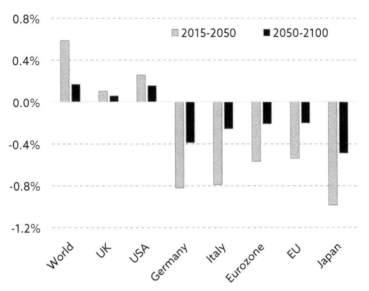

Source: United Nations (2015).

Note: EU numbers are ex. the UK. Data based on those aged 15–59.

You may wonder why, in exhibit 4.3, the EU workforce will decline marginally more than the Eurozone workforce in the years to come. After all, Italy and Germany are both members of the Eurozone, and both are badly affected by ageing.

Eastern Europe is the answer. It suffers from the worst demographic statistics in the entire world. The worst affected country of them all – Bulgaria – should see its workforce decline by 1.5% annually for many years to come. Adding to Bulgaria's predicament, Romania, Poland, Croatia and Hungary are all in a much worse condition than Germany or Italy.

What demographics can tell us

Back in 2012, Robert Arnott and Denis Chaves published what I believe is the most extensive study ever conducted on the effect on economic growth and financial market returns from changes in age distribution. Exhibits 4.4.1–4.4.3 are from that paper, and they deserve close inspection, as the results are highly significant; however, I need to explain how to read the charts.

Arnott and Chaves used 60 years of data across more than 100 countries in the study. The objective was to assess whether changes in the age-wise composition of the population has a significant effect on economic growth (exhibit 4.4.1), but Arnott and Chaves didn't stop there. They also analysed to what degree changing age distributions have affected equity returns (exhibit 4.4.2) and bond returns (exhibit 4.4.3). Returns were measured as excess returns over cash returns to adjust for the fact that the risk-free rate of return is vastly different across markets and time.

To better understand how to read the charts, I suggest you take a closer look at exhibit 4.4.1. The chart peaks at 0.15–0.20% for the 30–34 age cohort, meaning that a 1% higher concentration of 30–34 olds would lead to an *increase* in annual GDP growth of 0.15–0.20%. Likewise, a 1% higher concentration of the 70+ age cohort would lead to a *decrease* in annual GDP growth of 0.3–0.4%. Given the large number of baby boomers knocking on the 70+ door, these findings should not be ignored.

Exhibit 4.4.1: GDP growth vs. demographic shares

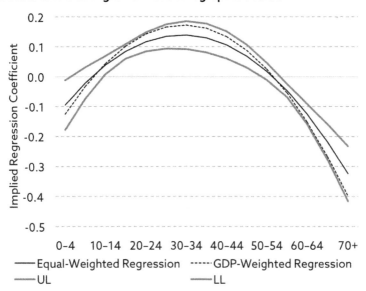

Exhibit 4.4.2: Equity returns vs. demographic shares

Exhibit 4.4.3: Bond returns vs. demographic shares

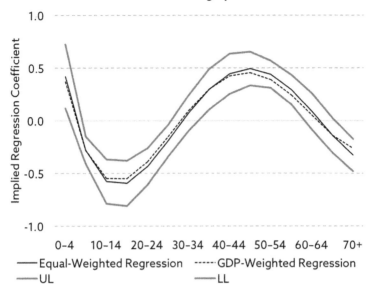

Note: UL = upper limit; LL = lower limit.

Arnott and Chaves sum up their findings better than I could ever do:

> "Children are not immediately helpful to GDP. They do not contribute to it, nor do they help stock and bond market returns in any meaningful way; their parents are likely disinvesting to pay their support. Young adults are the driving force in GDP growth; they are the sources of innovation and entrepreneurial spirit. But they are not yet investing; they are overspending against their future human capital. Middle-aged adults are the engine for capital market returns; they are in their prime for income, savings, and investments. And senior citizens contribute to neither GDP growth nor stock and bond market returns; they disinvest to buy goods and services that they no longer produce."

Other studies suggest households reduce their exposure to equities in a meaningful way as they grow older[45] – in line with Arnott and Chaves' conclusion that large cohorts of 70+ year olds imply difficult conditions for equities in the years ahead. We know that baby boomers account for 40% of US consumer spending, so their effect on the economy and financial markets should not come as a major surprise.

Before I move on, I should bring one more study to your attention. Back in 2011, the Federal Reserve Bank of San Francisco published a paper that demonstrated a powerful relationship between the age distribution of the US population and P/E ratios.

Using what they call the M/O ratio – which measures the middle-aged cohort (those aged 40–49) to the old-age cohort (those aged 60–69) – they predict US equity valuations to fall until the mid-2020s, where US P/E multiples should bottom out at 8–9 times earnings. Valuations are then projected to rise again (exhibit 4.5). The study found that the M/O ratio explains about 60% of the change in equity valuations over the past 60 years, which suggests quite a potent relationship.

---

45   See for example McKinsey & Company (2016,1).

Exhibit 4.5: Projected equity valuations from demographic trends

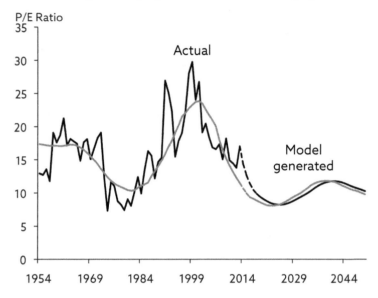

Source: Federal Reserve Bank of San Francisco (2011) .

Some thoughts on ageing and inflation

Having established that ageing is likely to affect economic growth as well as returns on bonds and equities negatively in the years to come, let's dig a little deeper on the impact ageing is likely to have on inflation, because that is not as straightforward as it first appears.

The prevailing view is that, other things being equal, inflation is likely to stay subdued as the number of elderly grow. As I have already noted, older consumers spend less than younger consumers do, which should hold back not only economic growth but also upward pressure on consumer prices.

That is precisely the conclusion most investors came to after we all saw what happened in Japan, as the world's oldest population aged. For many years, core CPI in Japan has been tightly correlated with the size of the local workforce (exhibit 4.6).

Exhibit 4.6: Japanese working age population vs. core CPI

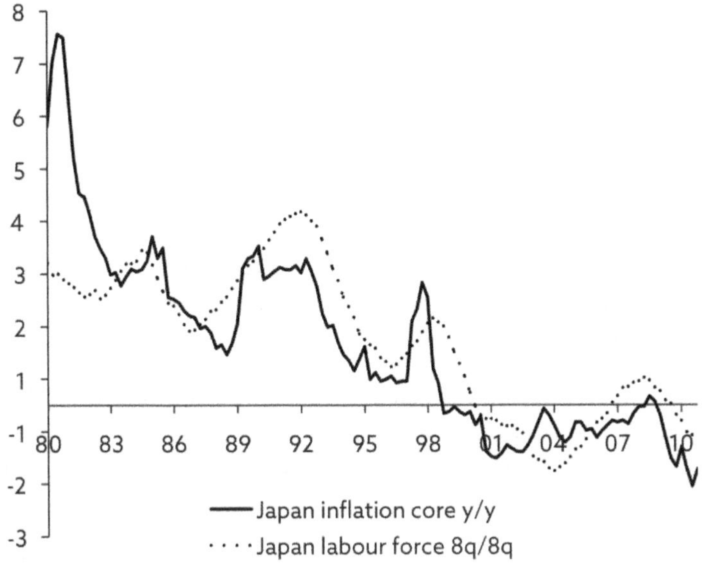

Source: Barclays Research (2014).

This has led many to conclude that it is only a matter of time before the Eurozone falls into the same trap.

But could we have all reached the wrong conclusion?

Could ageing possibly be inflationary? After all, Japan's status as a creditor nation, its next-to-zero immigration population and low female participation in the workforce makes it a less than optimal comparison to Europe and the US.

The BIS study

The Bank for International Settlements (BIS) came to a somewhat surprising conclusion, when their researchers took a closer look at the topic in 2015[46]. They found that, in many countries, inflation has moved largely in tandem with the dependency ratio, i.e. the more dependents, the higher the rate of inflation and vice versa.

I should point out that BIS' researchers used the dependency ratio – not the old-age dependency ratio – in their study. Could it possibly be that rising dependency ratios in the years to come will be driven by more youngsters rather than more old people? The answer is an unequivocal no.

Secondly, could it be that youngsters affect inflation much more than the elderly do? After all, it shouldn't come as a surprise to anyone that children are tremendously expensive. BIS looked at different age groups' impact on inflation and, although young people impact inflation more than the elderly do, BIS found the difference to be surprisingly modest.

Thirdly, could it be that it matters a great deal how old the elderly actually are? I know from other studies that people aged 70 spend a lot more money than those aged 85, and they spend it very differently. BIS didn't address this issue at all, but I will do so below.

Fourthly, economic factors and political factors can both drive the demographic impact on inflation. BIS made the point in its research study that, although both sets of factors have indeed impacted inflation over time, the effect from changing economic conditions is greater than that of political factors. This is important, as it makes BIS' findings more robust.

Finally, the spike in inflation in the late 1970s and early 1980s not only coincided with a peak in the dependency ratio. Oil prices also skyrocketed, which resulted in widespread inflation calamity. Is it possible that the apparent link between demographics and inflation is just a coincidence?

Is it possible that inflation is driven by economic factors like oil prices, and that the apparent link between inflation and the dependency ratio 35–40 years ago was driven by something entirely different? BIS tested

---

46   Bank for International Settlements (2015,1).

for this and found their results not only to be statistically significant but very robust.

I should also point out that, despite the robustness of BIS' findings, other research papers have arrived at different conclusions, and that many remain convinced that ageing is always disinflationary. One shouldn't assume that the BIS research paper is akin to the holy grail, but it certainly raises a question or two, and investors would be advised not to automatically adopt the view that ageing is always disinflationary, just because that is what happened in Japan.

Why does BIS think ageing is inflationary?

BIS offers a relatively simple explanation as to why more old people in society is likely to create inflationary headwinds. It is not that they spend more than everyone thinks they do. Older people definitely consume less than the younger generations, which is disinflationary. However, they consume a lot more than they produce (which is next to nothing), which is inflationary.

Think of it as a classic supply and demand model. Demand falls as consumers age, but supply falls more. BIS' argument is therefore a relative one, not an absolute one. The two curves simply meet at a different point, causing prices to rise. BIS expects the inflationary headwinds to prevail for a very long time to come – at least for the next 30 years in Europe.

I am not saying that BIS has figured it all out, and the rest of us are plain stupid but, if its findings are anywhere close to the actual outcome, the rather benign inflation environment of the last 35 years will reverse in the years to come, and we will enter a more challenging environment. The impact from rising dependency ratios will vary somewhat from country to country, but inflation will rise everywhere (exhibit 4.7).

Exhibit 4.7: Demography's impact on inflation – past and future

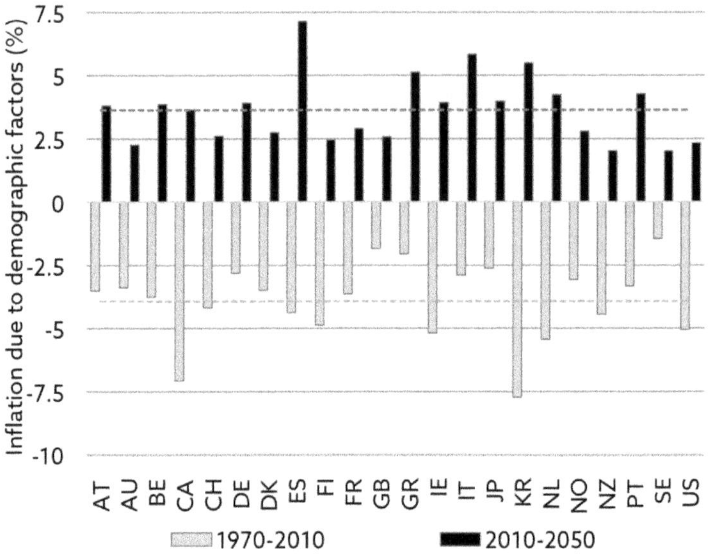

Source: BIS (2015,1).

Note 1: The dashed lines show averages of the above economies.

Note 2: The bars indicate accumulated inflationary pressure from demographic factors in the 1970–2010 period and expected accumulated inflation pressures in the 2010–2050 period respectively.

I should also point out that BIS' findings in no way imply that GDP growth will also confound expectations, just like inflation may do. Regardless of what happens to inflation, GDP growth is likely to stay muted for a long time to come. It is therefore not entirely unthinkable that we end up with a very unpleasant combination of low GDP growth and relatively high inflation – i.e. *stagflation*.

Total consumer spending by age group

Ageing affects consumer spending wherever you look. As you can see from exhibit 4.8, at least in the US (and I don't expect it to be much different elsewhere), income as well as consumer spending peaks when people are around 50 years old.

Exhibit 4.8: US income and expenditures by age group, 2013 (USD)

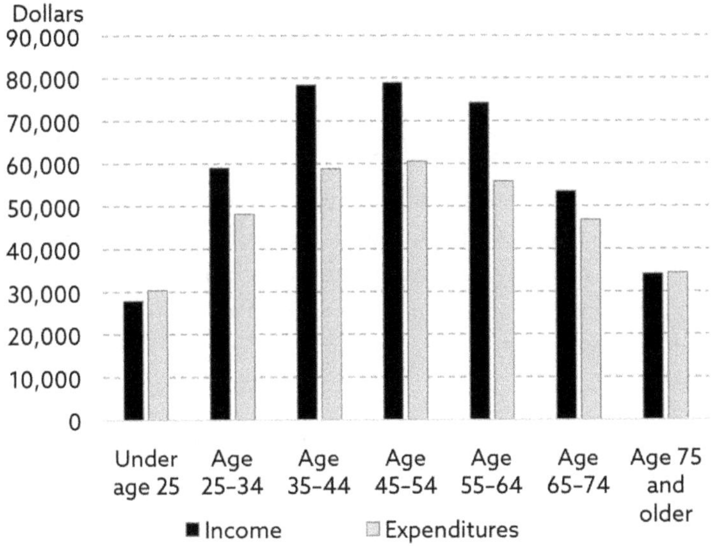

Source: Bureau of Labor Statistics (2015).

You won't be able to deduce this from exhibit 4.8, but spending peaks slightly later than income, and I think there is a good reason for that. Children typically move away from home when their parents are around 50, and suddenly those parents can afford goods and services they couldn't previously afford. The typical buyer of a Harley Davidson in the US is a man in his early 50s, and it is very much a function of this dynamic.

Once consumer spending has peaked, it falls modestly to begin with, but the decline in spending accelerates as people age. For example, the 55–64 year olds spend 7–8% less than those aged 45–54, but the 75+ year olds spend 26–27% less than the 65–74 olds, and only about half of the peak spenders. It is therefore only reasonable to assume that ageing's impact on economic growth will intensify in the years to come.

I should also point out that it is not only the more cyclical items such as cars, furniture, etc. that are impacted by ageing. Take food, one of the most stable consumer goods I can think of. Americans spend much less money on food as they age – at home as well as away from home. Having said that, the Japanese spend more on food as they age. Don't ask me why that is!

Ageing's effect on healthcare spending

Not surprisingly, anything healthcare related is very much in demand by the older generations. In the US, most healthcare spending is classified as consumer spending, as most healthcare is provided by the private sector over there. It goes down in the national accounts as government spending almost everywhere else, as healthcare is public in most countries.

This distinction is often a source of confusion. Whereas many believe that consumer spending is much higher in the US than it is in Europe, the difference is to a large degree explained by how healthcare spending is accounted for.

Given the forthcoming rise in the number of elderly, one would expect healthcare spending to account for a rising share of GDP almost everywhere, and that is precisely what will happen (exhibit 4.9). That said, it may surprise one or two that healthcare spending, when measured as a percentage of GDP, is likely to grow the fastest in the country with the most favourable demographics – the US. That is almost certainly a function of the US healthcare model, which is based on private care paid for by insurance companies, and that is indeed a very expensive model.

The researchers behind exhibit 4.9 calculated a best-fit trend (based on past data) on healthcare expenditures as a percentage of GDP for individual countries, then projected the trend forward to 2040, which resulted in the baseline case in exhibit 4.9. Meanwhile, the high case represents an assumption that future spending could accelerate slightly, given better treatment and higher patient expectations, leading to the 2040 high case.

Exhibit 4.9: Projected healthcare expenditures by 2040 (% of GDP)

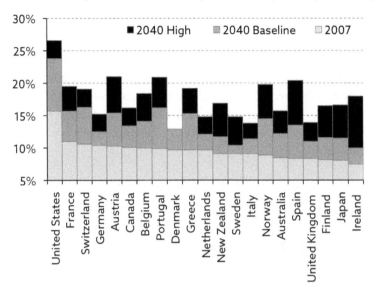

Source: World Economic Forum in collaboration with McKinsey & Company (2013).

In a study related to the study above, John Appleby looked at UK public health care (NHS) spending on behalf of the King's Fund[47], and his findings are truly frightening. If one assumes that healthcare spending (as a percentage of GDP) will continue to grow at the pace it grew in the first decade of the new millennium, then by the mid-2070s the NHS would be consuming close to 100% of UK GDP.

It goes without saying that something must give. 100% of GDP consumed by the NHS is clearly not sustainable. It is even more frightening when you think about the global context. The UK suffers from one of the least punishing demographic profiles. If that profile

---

47   King's Fund (2013).

translates into something as bad as that, I can only imagine what countries such as Germany or Italy can expect.

Why the US outlook is much better than that of Europe

As I have already pointed out, it does make a substantial difference to total consumer spending, and hence to GDP growth, how old the elderly actually are. A 70-year old still travels the world, whereas a 90-year old does not. In Japan, almost 8% of the populace are now over 80 years old, a number which will rise to approximately 15% by 2050 (exhibit 4.10).

Exhibit 4.10: People aged 80 and over in selected countries (% of total)

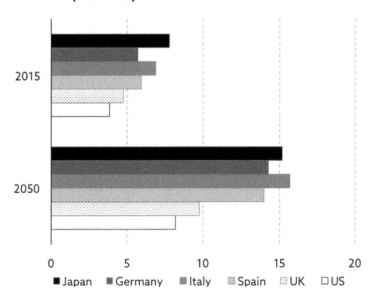

Source: United Nations (2015).

Most of Europe is still far behind Japan in terms of the number of elderly but, as you can see from exhibit 4.10, some of the largest

European countries will be catching up over the next few decades. By 2050, Italy will have more people aged 80 and older than Japan will.

Of the major European countries, only the UK and France are not facing such a dramatic rise in the number of elderly, although it is bad enough as it is in those countries. The only conclusion I can reach is that the Japanese 'disease' will almost certainly spread to Europe, if it hasn't already done so.

Looking ahead, the elderly will not account for such a big share of the overall population in the US as they will here in Europe, and the reason is simple. US baby boomers had, for reasons unknown to me, more children than European baby boomers had.

When mankind produces a generation as rich in numbers as the baby boom generation did, it is only natural to expect their offspring also to be relatively large in numbers, and that is precisely what has happened in the US. The children of the baby boomers have been named the echo boomers, and they will affect US economic growth positively, beginning in the mid-2020s.

Could I possibly be too pessimistic on Europe?

There is an obvious reason why the German government has repeatedly voiced a willingness to take more refugees than any other European country has. The German workforce will shrink dramatically between now and 2050, and the political leadership in Germany realise (unlike many political leaders in the UK) that they will need an influx of people, if they want to keep German industry alive.

Should other EU countries begin to adopt Germany's approach to migration, or should the retirement age be changed *meaningfully* (which is being discussed across Europe at present), the EU workforce may not drop as dramatically as projected in exhibit 4.3, and my gloomy projections for GDP growth in the EU may prove overly pessimistic.

Changing the retirement age has been a political hot potato in my home country, Denmark, for several years. Some political leaders, who can see the writing on the wall, have proposed a gradual rise of the retirement age, but the unions have screamed and yelled, as if there is no tomorrow. What these people don't seem to understand – or don't want to understand – is that the alternative to working a few years more is much worse.

Investment implications

The cost of dying is excessive and society will soon be forced to change the current practice of paying for healthcare with few questions asked. From an investment point of view, the implication is that some healthcare strategies will likely do much better than others going forward. Pricing will most likely be increasingly regulated, and one should therefore be particularly cautious with healthcare strategies that depend on aggressive pricing to succeed.

The US Census Bureau provides very detailed information as to when (i.e. at what age) spending peaks on various goods and services. For example, spending on the very first car peaks at the age of 25, and the US consumer is 84 when spending peaks on nursing home services[48].

This information, when combined with the knowledge that the largest age group in the US is the 45–54 cohort, can be used by investors to position their portfolio correctly and/or to make the necessary adjustments as people age. Phrased differently, given the demographic outlook, and based on the information provided, investors would probably be foolish to invest in secondhand car dealerships or suppliers of infant furniture.

New cars or motorcycles are more likely to be in demand over the next few years, and so is anything home-related, as people begin to upgrade their home quite late in life. All the china that was smashed years ago by

---

48   Source: Harry S Dent (2014).

those unruly children is replaced, which will provide the grandchildren with an opportunity to do the same, but that is a different story.

Later again, the emphasis switches to life insurance, retirement homes, cruise ship holidays, and driver-less cars, not to mention anything healthcare related. Obviously, this is a process that has already begun, but the big wave – the tsunami – is still in front of us.

Exhibit 4.11: Consumption levels by age group, 1984–2013 (USD)

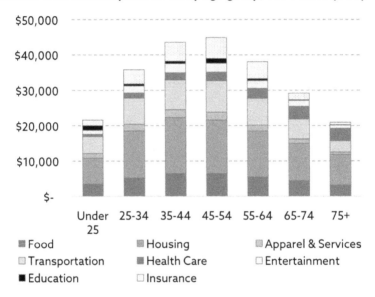

Source: Haver Analytics, Bureau of Labor Statistics, Morgan Stanley Wealth Management Investment Resources (2017). Copyright © 2017 Morgan Stanley Smith Barney LLC.

Exhibit 4.11 provides a good overview as to how spending changes over life, as consumers age. The chart only covers consumption spending in the US, but I wouldn't expect spending patterns to be materially different in other developed countries, except for the total amount spent on food by the elderly in Japan!

One word of caution to wrap up this chapter. Although I believe there is plenty of evidence to suggest that the greying of the baby boomers will have a rather dramatic impact on the economy and financial markets in the years to come, the fact that a study is statistically significant (which the studies referred to in this book all are) does not necessarily imply that it can be trusted to accurately predict the future. In a rapidly changing, and increasingly global, environment, can one realistically expect behavioural patterns of yesteryear to be repeated? Only time can tell.

This implies that one needs to interpret the output of these sorts of studies with care. A simple example: almost without exception, the largest companies in the world today are truly global in nature and depend only modestly on their home market.

The fact that Switzerland will age rapidly over the next 15 years means much less to Nestle now than it did 30 years ago. One therefore needs to look not only at each and every country in terms of where it is in the demographic food chain, but also at the constituents making up the local stock market.

5

The Declining Spending Power of the Middle Classes

The Brits decided to leave the EU. The Americans chose a political outsider as their next president. 2016 turned into a political minefield, and the reason is obvious. Many feel under extreme financial pressure. Wages are no longer growing in real terms, and have even started to decline in some countries. The global middle classes, who effectively underwrite political and economic stability, want something to change, whatever that something is. I will look at the economic ramifications of that, and how governments could – and should – respond.

The declining spending power[49]

MANY ANGLO-SAXONS SAVE little. They live from paycheque to paycheque to make ends meet, and their living standards are very much a function of their ability to hold on to their job *and* their ability

---

[49] Coming from Denmark, I almost take for granted that 95% of the populace all over the developed world belong to the middle classes, as is the case in my country, but that is obviously not correct. In other words, when I use the term middle classes, bear in mind that I had my Danish glasses on when writing this book. For a more precise definition of those affected by falling real wages, look at the McKinsey study later in this chapter.

to negotiate regular pay rises. There is no cushion to speak of, should anything untoward happen.

If that happens, the writing is on the wall. Living standards stagnate or even decline. According to a new study[50], 78% of all US workers live this way. It is not quite so dramatic in the UK, but the number is still high.

Here is the problem. Across the world, many who live this way have experienced a drop in real wages in recent years, so even if the overall employment situation is quite robust, as there are no savings to fall back on, many have suffered a fall in living standards.

The decline in real wage growth started all the way back in the 1970s and has coincided with an increase in corporate profits. More recently the trend has gained momentum, though, to the extent that real wages are now falling in some countries, which has had the effect of suppressing aggregate consumer demand even further.

Considering consumer spending's impact on GDP growth, if the growth in real wages started to slow down more than 40 years ago, it is hardly a surprise that the growth in GDP has also slowed over those 40 years.

The force is not with us

I was born at the tail-end of the baby boom. I consider myself less fortunate than my parents, both of whom were born in 1935. My parents are no different from most other parents of their generation. Entirely consistent with Modigliani's life-cycle hypothesis, my parents didn't start saving for their retirement until they reached their mid-40s. That effectively gave my father a good 20 years to ensure that he and my mum can enjoy their retirement without worrying too much about money.

My parents were lucky, because they started saving in earnest in the early 1980s, at the outset of what would become the biggest bull market

---

50   Conducted by CareerBuilder (2017).

of all time and, by the time things got wobbly, they were home and dry. Over those two decades, a global equity portfolio generated a total inflation-adjusted return of about 850%[51].

Unfortunately, not everyone has been that privileged. My generation has only been saving for the last couple of decades, and many are still underwater on investments they had when hell broke loose in 2008. I, together with hundreds of millions of other baby boomers across the world, am now chasing whatever returns I can find to ensure that my retirement can be enjoyed in relative comfort like my parents'. But the force is not with us.

The truth

Back to the question I raised in chapter 1:

Why has everything lost momentum?

To fully understand that, I suggest you take another look at exhibits 1.1.1–1.1.4. As I pointed out in chapter 1, productivity growth, GDP growth (both in nominal and in real terms), inflation and interest rates have all trended down for a very long time – by most accounts since the 1970s.

In microeconomic theory, the price (P) and quantity (Q) that a company can achieve on its goods and services is a function of where demand (D) meets supply (S) which, in geometric terms, is where the two lines cross each other in exhibit 5.1. Let's call that equilibrium A, with the shaded area under A being equal to $P \times Q$.

---

51 In USD terms.

Exhibit 5.1: Geometric interpretation of GDP growth

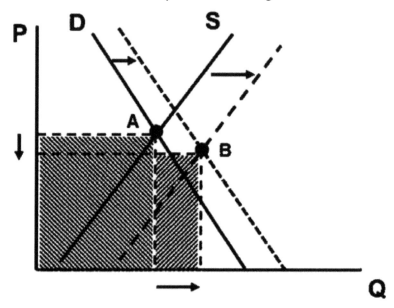

Source: Strategic Economic Decisions (2016).

Now, assume both S and D move out as the economy grows (as they do), but that D moves out more slowly than S for reasons I will come back to later. The shaded area under the new equilibrium B is the new P×Q.

P×Q, when aggregated across the economy, is a proxy for total output (GDP) in the private sector. In other words, the shaded area under A is a geometric illustration of GDP before S and D change, and the shaded area under B represents GDP after S and D have changed. The difference between the two shaded areas equals the change in GDP (ΔGDP) in the private sector.

It follows from this that, as per microeconomic theory, any change to private sector GDP is a function of changes in either supply or demand (or both). Hence the obvious conclusion – if the aim is to boost private sector GDP growth, one must establish conditions that allow D to move out faster than S.

Why the S-curve has shifted out faster than the D-curve

Before I suggest possible solutions to this, let me offer at least a couple of reasons why the supply curve (the S-curve) has shifted out faster than the demand curve (the D-curve) since the 1970s. The question you need to ask yourself is the following – did anything fundamental change around that time? Has anything been different in the years since the 1970s when compared to what it was like before then?

It is certainly not demographics, as they were very supportive of demand throughout the 1980s and 1990s, when the baby boomers moved into their peak spending years. What could it be then? To understand this rather unique phenomenon you need to know that, in the national accounts, national income is ultimately shared between labour and capital. Wages and bonuses make up labour's share, and everything else (corporate profits, dividends, interest income, etc.) is classified as capital income.

You also need to know that, ever since economic statistics were introduced in a more systematic fashion in the early 20th century, labour has taken a near constant share of national income. The British economist Arthur Bowley was the first to observe this regularity, and thus it became known as Bowley's Law.

In the 1920s, the American economist Paul Douglas made a similar finding in the US and developed, together with the mathematician Charles Cobb, the now famous Cobb-Douglas production function, which has led a whole host of other economists to conclude that the income distribution between capital and labour is virtually constant.

That is precisely how it worked until the 1970s. Then things began to unravel. Year after year, labour lost a little bit to capital (on average about 0.3% per year) and, although the accumulated loss since 1970 is quite different from country to country, almost all countries have seen a meaningful chunk of what used to be labour income going into the pockets of capital owners (exhibit 5.2). This would again (at least partly) explain the extraordinary strength of the equity bull market since the early 1980s.

Exhibit 5.2: Change in labour's share of national income in various countries, 1970–2014

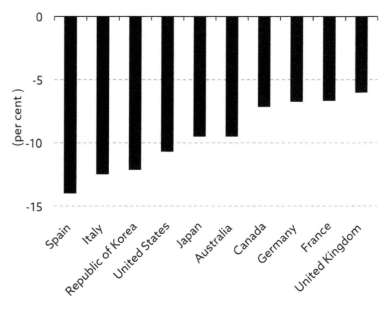

Source: OECD (2015).

It is not a phenomenon that only applies to the more mature countries. Most emerging market (EM) countries have experienced the same[52], leading labour to lose out to capital globally. This has led to what is frequently called the elephant chart (exhibit 5.3). If you take a closer look, I am sure you can see the resemblance with an elephant.

As is evident from that chart, the middle classes of the developed world have been the biggest losers over the past few decades. Their income growth in the 1988–2008 period was negative and, even more remarkably, it was lower than that of the world's poorest.

---

[52] OECD (2015) provides more detail on this phenomenon.

Exhibit 5.3: Global income growth, 1988–2008

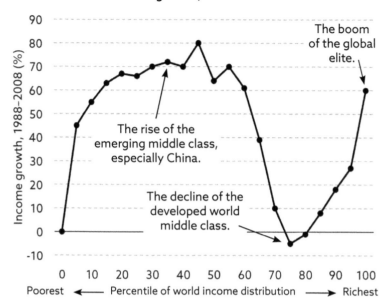

Source: World Bank (2012).

Meanwhile, EM middle classes have done very well, and so have the global elite. No wonder the man in the street is not particularly happy these days. Whether governments are prepared to address the problem is an altogether different question.

Poorer than your parents?

Let me share some bad news with you. If we do nothing, the D-curve will most likely continue to shift out more slowly than the S-curve, prices will begin to fall more broadly, and GDP growth will ultimately turn negative.

Why is that?

Assume that (i) the D-curve is always downward-sloping (as it is), (ii) the S-curve is always upward-sloping (as it is), (iii) S shifts out faster than D over time (as it has done for years), and (iv) both the S-curve and the D-curve are linear (as they are most of the time).

Based on those reasonable assumptions, it can be proven mathematically that GDP growth will conform to a downward-opening parabola (exhibit 5.4), and that it will ultimately turn negative. In other words, it is not entirely unrealistic that, if we choose to sit on our hands – and in that context QE and other means of monetary policy is akin to doing nothing – not only could the stagnation of recent years continue for a long time to come, but prices may start to decline more broadly, and GDP growth may turn negative – very much like in the 1930s.

Exhibit 5.4: GDP growth when supply shifts out faster than demand

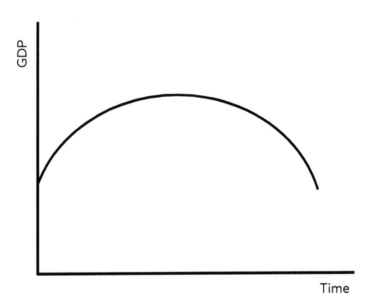

Source: Strategic Economic Decisions (2016).

Although national income is always shared between capital and labour in a broadly similar manner, I should point out that it is not distributed evenly, and the split varies from country to country. In the largest economy of them all, the USA, two-thirds of national income used to go to labour and one-third to capital. Labour's share has since dropped to just over 60%.

Meanwhile, in the UK, labour used to take almost 75% of national income; that has since dropped to just over 70%. This may explain the extraordinarily good times equity investors have enjoyed over the past 35 years or so, but it also explains why the aggregate D-curve has shifted out more slowly than it used to.

The McKinsey study

McKinsey Global Institute has, to the best of my knowledge, done the most comprehensive study so far on the declining income trend. In a study from the summer of 2016[53], they concluded that 65–70% of all households in 25 advanced countries – or 540–580 million people – were in a segment of the income distribution whose real market incomes[54] were either stagnating or in decline in 2014 when compared to 2005. By comparison, only 2% – or less than 10 million people – experienced the same between 1993 and 2005.

Lower tax rates and rising transfer payments have reduced the impact. When taking those factors into account, 'only' 20–25% have suffered either stagnating or declining disposable income. However, that also (at least partly) explains why government debt continues to rise.

Italy has been particularly badly affected by this trend with no less than 97% of the population belonging to households that have suffered from stagnating or even declining incomes. The corresponding numbers in the US and the UK are 81% and 70% respectively. Across advanced economies, the average is 65–70%, but the variation is dramatic. Take Sweden, where only 20% have experienced anything like that.

---

53 Source: McKinsey & Company (2016,2).
54 McKinsey Global Institute defines real market income as the sum of wages and income from capital.

The impact of globalisation and low interest rates

It is therefore only fair to conclude that the D-curve has been held back by stagnating or declining incomes across the developed world. Meanwhile, the S-curve has shifted out relatively fast – partly because of better technology (digitalisation, etc.) and partly because of globalisation. If you think back, you will probably remember how life was different back in the 1970s. China was not yet on the international trade map, and most manufacturing companies did all their manufacturing back home.

The picture today is very different with international trade accounting for a much bigger share of economic activity than it did in the 1970s. It is a sad state of affairs that globalisation, which is just another way to describe international trade, is rapidly becoming an F-word. Few trends have benefitted economic growth more than international trade.

Adding to all of that, let me offer another reason why the S-curve has shifted out so fast. Exceedingly low interest rates have kept inefficient businesses alive. Such businesses would under normal circumstances have been wiped out rather quickly, but low interest rates have acted as a life support machine, and the net result is a more rapidly shifting S-curve across the world.

Summing it all up, both the D-curve and the S-curve have changed momentum but in opposite directions. It is therefore no surprise that the equilibrium point between supply and demand has moved a fair bit.

How to boost aggregate demand

Policy makers' choice of policy model – monetary policy – is one that will never fix this problem; policy makers need to realise once and for all that monetary policy has no meaningful impact on the D-curve. If anything, access to cheap capital amongst corporates has allowed the S-curve to shift out more rapidly than the D-curve.

Monetary policy – and QE in particular – served an important purpose in the immediate aftermath of the financial crisis, but central bankers have allowed it to become a quasi-permanent feature, and that is a mistake.

To begin with, policy makers must distinguish between the private and the public sectors:

➻ In the *private sector*, there is only one way to re-accelerate economic growth, and that is to establish conditions for demand to shift out faster than supply and,

➻ in the *public sector*, it is all about increasing government spending (in an intelligent way).

Let's begin with the private sector.

Is it possible to enhance the spending power of the public without turning it into a socialist economy?

The answer is yes – think helicopter money. But certainly not Zimbabwe-style helicopter money, which was an unmitigated disaster not that many years ago. Think of it instead as helicopter money delivered through fiscal means and designed to increase the spending power of the poorest two-thirds of income earners.

One way this could be achieved will be revealed in chapter 10; however, before you object to spending public money on non-productivity-enhancing initiatives like helicopter money, think about the trillions of dollars that companies from all over the world have stashed away in offshore tax havens. Taxing that money at a reasonable rate could easily finance such a policy, and pushing out the D-curve would benefit the corporate sector anyway.

What else could we do?

Some will argue that de-globalisation could also do the trick, but I won't even go there. Such a move would be a very unfortunate step back into the dark ages and would totally disregard the contribution that rising international trade has made to economic growth over the past few decades.

In the public sector, as already mentioned, it is all about increasing spending. Increase government spending, and economic growth will be boosted instantaneously. Our vote-hungry political leadership tend to favour bribing the electorate by boosting transfer payments, but the multiplier on transfer payments is very low, and the impact on productivity is non-existent.

Politicians should instead focus on productivity-enhancing infrastructure projects, just like Eisenhower did when he came back from the war in Europe. Building more and better highways, as Eisenhower did, is not the way forward, but high-speed – and affordable – internet access most definitely is.

Will it happen?

Almost certainly yes as far as increased infrastructure spending is concerned. There appears to be a drive towards that in both the UK and the US. That said, are the governments currently in power likely to boost aggregate demand by putting more money into the hands of the bottom two-thirds of income earners? With conservative powers in charge in many countries, I doubt that will happen anytime soon, but it will most likely happen eventually.

If the fall in real wages continues (and it will unless governments take drastic action), the electorate will become more and more desperate for things to change, and Brexit and Trump will only be the beginning of much worse to come[55]. Opposition parties in many countries have an outstanding opportunity to put this right and, in the eyes of the middle classes, be the true heroes, but few seem to understand the issue at stake here.

---

[55] Many will tell you that Brexit was not about falling real wages but about border controls. At first glance, that is correct, but why do you think people want stricter border controls? Because they feel increasingly insecure as living standards are dropping.

Furthermore, economic laws don't change just because the president of the United States happens to be a successful businessman, or because the UK political arena is in such disarray. When the penny finally drops, and the political leadership begin to realise that there is no alternative to increasing the spending power of the public, the party in global equity markets is likely over.

Investment implications

The most obvious investment opportunities in the years to come, should governments switch from an emphasis on monetary policy to fiscal policy, are to be found in the infrastructure space and, considering the dilapidated state of the infrastructure in both the UK and the US, there should be plenty of opportunities on offer.

Let me give you just one example. If (when) tariffs are raised on international trades[56], shipping goods as cheaply as possible would become more important than ever. Low-cost shipping implies larger container ships, though, and many container ports are not deep enough to facilitate the largest containerships now in operation.

This means that there will be plenty of excavation work to come in container ports around the world, and it will be up to the government in question to ensure that returns on those infrastructure projects are high enough to attract capital from institutional investors. Once the UK has left the EU, a number of UK ports will be prime candidates for work of this nature.

In the private sector, if governments find ways to increase the momentum of aggregate demand growth, equities could perform quite well for a time – at least until investors realise that the increase in aggregate demand has come at the cost of reduced corporate profit growth.

---

[56] Whether the UK government is prepared to admit it or not, trade tariffs will increase if there is no free trade agreement between the EU and the UK.

The big losers, should all this materialise, will be anyone exposed to rising interest rates. In that context, I would worry mostly about the property market. It is quite scary how many people have bought property in recent years, not based on what they can afford, should mortgage rates rise to the long-term average rate, but based on what they can afford when they pay next to nothing in interest.

I cannot help reminding these people that I paid 18% on the very first mortgage I had back in 1981, and 5% would be *nothing*. Mortgage rates could rise to 5% in no time. I am not saying they will, but they could, and house buyers' attitude towards risk management today is bordering on negligence.

The big loser, should none of this happen, will be us all. Brexit and Trump are only the first signs that we are moving into an environment resembling that of the 1930s, and should the economy go into a secular reverse, there are unpleasant times to come.

One more point, which will be discussed in more detail in chapter 12, but let me whet your appetite now. If (when) labour start to grab a bigger share of national income, as I said earlier, the obvious consequence will be a drop in corporate profit growth, and that will almost certainly hurt equity returns. In such an environment, investors should not aim for respectable returns on their portfolio through equity beta exposure but through other means, but more about this in chapter 12.

6

The Rise of the East

My good friend and mentor, Woody Brock, encouraged me to write this chapter. He provided much of the content, and he inspired me to think of the growing role of China in a somewhat different context, which I am about to share with you. The rise of the East could be bad for the West, but it is also a structural trend that contains several positive aspects, which investors can benefit from.

The opportunity set

THE FIRST TIME I turned my attention to this topic was when, years ago, I read in the *Independent* newspaper that Afghan poppy growers had begun to switch from opium to wheat. Something must be astray for that to happen, I said to myself, so I began to investigate and an interesting story unfolded.

I realised that whilst the political establishment focused, and continue to focus, on climate change, a tsunami, also known as the global food crisis, began to develop and is now threatening to undermine political and economic stability in large parts of the world. I am not at all suggesting that climate change is not a serious issue. It certainly is, and it could quite possibly do severe damage to the world as we know it, but it would be a grave mistake to underestimate the pending food crisis.

According to at least one estimate[57], mankind is facing a formidable challenge. Between now and 2050, we will need to produce more food than we have done in the previous 10,000 years put together, and that is very much a function of rising livings standards across emerging markets – particularly in Asia.

When living standards are low, diets are simple and cheap. We know from various episodes of famine in Europe that people can survive on potatoes for a very long time, and many people around the world survive on rice to this day.

According to the World Bank, more than one billion people around the world survive on as little as $1–2 per day, and people in the poorest countries spend nearly 80% of their income on food. Meanwhile, at the other end of the scale, only 6–7% of total consumer expenditures in the US is spent on food products, whereas the typical OECD country would spend 10–15%[58].

We know that income per capita across emerging markets is likely to rise dramatically in the years to come, and we know that, when poor people have more money to spend, the very first thing they spend it on is more and better food. Consequently, if history repeats itself, demand for protein-rich food such as meat will rise exponentially in the years to come.

At the same time, the supply curve is also changing. As urban areas expand, arable land continues to disappear. Take Africa; in 1950, only 15% of Africa's population lived in urban areas. By 2000, that number had risen to 33% and, by 2030, 55% of Africa's population are expected to live in urban areas[59].

---

57   Source: *The Economist* (2015).
58   I would not for one second suggest that the average American is better off economically than the average Western European; the difference in food spending between the two continents is simply a function of different food cultures. The take-away culture keeps US food spending down, as money spent on restaurants and take-aways is not included in these numbers.
59   Source: United Nations (2014).

My point is a simple one. As living standards rise across emerging markets, the percentage of total consumer spending that goes towards food drops, but food spending when measured in absolute terms rises noticeably, and the quality of the food that is consumed also rises. This provides investment opportunities for investors thinking outside-the-box (more about this later).

Adding to that dynamic, changing demographics cause another challenge – but also an opportunity. The average farmer in most developed countries is now in his late 50s and, in many cases, his children either cannot afford to take over the farm, or they have no desire to do so. A new farming model is therefore required. Farming will increasingly become a corporate business.

How I define the East

When reading about the subject, you often get the impression that East means China but, in reality, there is a lot more to the Asian story than just China. Although China is likely to overtake the US economy in the not so distant future and become the largest (and most powerful?) economy on earth, many other countries stand to benefit.

Having said that, when is it likely to happen and what are the implications? Equally importantly, as we have learned over the years, power is not only about economic power. Which other sources of power determine a country's overall power? And, in the context of power, how do the other Asian countries fit into the China story? Although those countries do not possess the sheer might of China, the impact on (and of) other Asian countries should not be underestimated.

One could go one step further and define East as emerging markets (EM) more broadly, but that raises a whole host of other issues. When I think of EM, I think of Latin America, Eastern Europe, Africa and parts of Asia. One could argue that China is such a unique story that it should stand alone from that of the rest of Asia.

The emerging market story is therefore in reality four, or maybe even five, different stories. The problem with that approach is that the five stories are *massively* different; they are subject to such different dynamics that to pretend it is one story is simply a non-starter.

For all these reasons, my definition of the East would include China as well as all those countries throughout Asia that stand to benefit from the China growth story. I would even incorporate Australia in that story, although I am very aware that Australia is not even an Asian country.

The meaning of power

What does it mean to say that China is likely to become the most powerful economy?

To answer that question, and to understand the ramifications, I need to go back to the developers of game theory, John Nash and John Harsanyi, for a minute. In game theory, and in the context of bargaining, there are four sources of overall power:

1. **Economic power.** All other things being equal, the greater your economic power is, the greater your overall power is. Nash and Harsanyi labelled it resource endowment.

2. **Risk tolerance.** The greater your risk tolerance is, relative to the risk tolerance of whoever you are bargaining with, the greater your overall power is.

3. **Threat power.** In game theory, the greater your threat power is, i.e. your ability to inflict damage on the opposition, the greater your overall power is.

4. **Coalition power.** In a bargaining situation, if you can gain support from other powers (players in game theory), you boost your own overall power.

These four sources of power define your overall power in bilateral bargaining.

Economic power is shifting from West to East

With respect to the first of the four sources of power, economic power is a combination of the sheer might of the economy in question and how fast it is growing. The US economy is still much larger than the Chinese economy, but the latter is growing faster; hence the point I made earlier that it is only a question of time before China's economic power is bigger than that of the US.

The Chinese continue to inflate their economic growth rate in lean times (or so the insiders tell me). Despite 2015 being by far the most difficult year in China in recent times, Chinese GDP continued to grow 7%. You probably shouldn't believe that number, but neither should you believe the growing army of China bashers in the West who remain convinced that the China growth story is one big fraud.

I have friends and business acquaintances who regularly meet with people in high positions in China, and they have told me that the Chinese economy probably grew by 3–4% in 2015, even if it felt like a recession as it came on the back of years of very strong economic growth. My point is a slightly different one. If 3–4% GDP growth is the low point of the economic cycle, you'd better take China seriously. This is an economic monster being created.

Admittedly, you get different numbers depending on who you speak to, but my sources have all delivered essentially the same verdict. They tell me that the Chinese may be guilty of smoothing the figures but that, over the long term, official numbers are not too far from the true numbers.

Allow me to go back to the Industrial Revolution in the West, which created outsized economic growth for an extended period of time. Between 1830 and 1900, GDP quadrupled in the UK – a growth rate that has never since been matched in the West.

By comparison, in just 26 years leading up to the Global Financial Crisis, Chinese GDP grew tenfold. Quite extraordinary and without comparison to anything we have ever experienced before. Even if you take a few percentage points off recent years' growth rates, economic growth in China still easily outpaces the growth rate the West experienced through the Industrial Revolution. I can therefore comfortably say that, at least as far as economic power is concerned, the East is on the rise.

Some further thoughts on economic power

As already stated, economic power is a function of the size of the economic engine, but also a function of how fast it is growing. As discussed already, at the most fundamental level, economic growth is the sum of how fast the workforce is growing (or shrinking), and how much the output per hour changes, which brings us back to the simple equation I introduced earlier in the book:

$$\Delta GDP = \Delta Workforce + \Delta Productivity$$

In practical terms, though, several factors affect output. Economic growth theory was first developed by Robert Solow whilst at MIT back in the 1950s. He assumed that total output was a function of three variables. In addition to the contribution from changes in the workforce, he also assumed that capital and land affect output, both of which are an implicit part of ΔProductivity in the equation above.

Consequently, he developed the following production function:

$$GDP = f(W,C,L) + e$$

where W denotes the workforce, C is capital, L is land, and e is the noise coming from missing factors.

Paul Romer of Stamford University further developed this simple production function. He introduced innovation (I) to the equation, and he introduced a subscript **t**, indicating that all the factors change over time. Consequently, the production function changed to:

$$GDP = f_t(W,C,L,I) + e$$

Subsequent work has concluded that a whole host of non-quantifiable factors also affect economic growth – the quality of the educational system, the legal system and government regulations to mention a few. Economists have labelled these factors as one and call them the *incentive structure* (IS). The production function has consequently changed as follows:

$$GDP = f_t(W,C,L,I,IS) + e$$

In the context of this book, adding IS to the production function is important, because governments can impact the incentive structure, whereas they cannot impact the other factors much.

Economic growth has been miserable in recent years and, whereas some people argue that it is all down to this or that, I would argue that the true reason is rather more complex. Take one input factor that is often blamed for the current misery – poor demographics.

Yes, we do face demographic headwinds and, yes, negative demographics have already had some impact on economic growth but, realistically, much worse is to come. However, governments have not made it any easier by creating sub-optimal incentive structures.

A bad incentive structure – an example from real life

A simple but important example: going into the Global Financial Crisis, various European governments had made it far too difficult for corporates to shrink their workforce in lean times, and corporates responded in kind. If you cannot fire, you don't hire. That is indeed one of the key reasons European job creation, and GDP growth, has been dramatically below that of the US in recent years.

A friend of mine ran a construction business in the Balearic island of Mallorca. As the Global Financial Crisis hit, and construction activity in Mallorca was wiped out for a while, he wanted to downsize his workforce. Far too much red tape forced him to close his business instead. The saddest part of the story is that politicians never seem to learn. Although Spanish labour laws have changed somewhat, employees hired when the old law applied are still subject to the old rules. In other words, there is still far too much red tape in Europe, and Spain is not the only country making that mistake.

Governments all over the world need to realise that the *only* factor in the production function above that they can influence to a meaningful degree is the incentive structure (IS). Legal systems must be simplified, labour markets must be de-regulated, corruption must be eliminated, marginal income tax rates – particularly low and middle-income rates – must come down, and we must educate our young people better. A lot can still be achieved, but only if our political leaders appreciate that this is the only way forward.

When will China outgrow the US?

If the US workforce grows 0.25% annually in the years to come (and we know that to be broadly accurate unless US immigration laws are fundamentally changed), and assuming productivity grows about 1% annually (which is perhaps a tad optimistic when looking at productivity improvements in recent years), US GDP should grow about 1.25% per year between now and 2050.

Whilst there is little risk attached to my workforce growth estimate, I could be way off on the productivity estimate I use in my projections. On the negative side, productivity is likely to fall further as debt continues to rise and the workforce ages. On the positive side, increased automation in the years to come could drive productivity higher.

Annual productivity gains have averaged about 1% over the very long term. As I pointed out back in chapter 1, since World War II, productivity has only grown significantly faster than that twice. In both those instances, annual productivity gains popped to 2–2.5% for 5–10 years before reverting to the long-term average.

As productivity could be impacted both negatively and positively in the years to come, using past averages as my base case doesn't seem unreasonable. However, given the Trump administration's appetite for infrastructure investing, US GDP growth should benefit, so I have taken the liberty to bump up my base case for US GDP growth to 1.5% annually.

I have chosen to use 2.5% annual GDP growth as my best case and 1% as my worst case. The numbers are not symmetrical around my base case, as I think Trump and subsequent US presidents will increase public spending quite dramatically, should GDP growth drop below 1%.

In that context, I ought to say that actual GDP growth, when measured from one year to the next, can be vastly different and will very much depend on cyclical factors. My numbers are estimates of the annualised average rate of growth when measured over the long term.

In the case of China, I have taken a different approach – partly because I don't have access to stats on China that provide the same level of detail and partly because, as I have already discussed, I don't fully trust the stats coming out of Beijing.

My starting point is 2015. If the Chinese economy could grow 3–4% in a particularly challenging year, 3% average annual GDP growth in the years to come becomes my worst case. My China sources tell me that, when China fires on all cylinders, annual GDP growth is probably around 7–8% when adjusted for inflation. Consequently, 7% is my best case, and the halfway point becomes my base case.

On that basis, and as you can see from exhibit 6.1, China is likely to catch up with the US in 2034 (using the base case in both instances). Admittedly, I have made no adjustments for purchasing power parities. On a PPP-adjusted basis, China's GDP could be higher than that of the US less than 10 years from now.

Exhibit 6.1: Chinese GDP catch-up under various assumptions

		Annual Chinese GDP Growth		
		3.00%	5.00%	7.00%
Annual US GDP Growth	1.00%	2047	2032	2027
	1.50%	2057	2034	2028
	2.50%	n/a	2041	2030

Source: Absolute Return Partners LLP

Other sources of power

If the anticipated shift in economic power from West to East is not that many years away, neither may we be far away from a shift in overall power. That view is further reinforced when looking at the other sources of power.

Since the Global Financial Crisis, risk tolerance in the West has been in decline. In the US, recent administrations have clearly been more risk-averse than what used to be the case, although President Trump seems to be willing to reverse that trend.

European governments, which have been noticeably more risk-averse than US administrations for many years, haven't exactly picked up the baton left behind by the US under Obama. Take Africa – while both Europe and the US have struggled in the aftermath of the Global Financial Crisis, China has roamed freely in Africa, pretty much unchallenged.

Looking forward, as people age and demand for social welfare programmes rise, I would fully expect risk tolerance to continue to decline. Domestic challenges will simply reduce the West's appetite for risk internationally.

As a natural consequence of falling risk tolerance, the threat power is also in decline. Under President Obama, the US made an unusually low number of credible threats (ISIS kept them busy), and a very risk-averse Europe made virtually none. Meanwhile, China was busy making credible threats in Asia. In 2011, China collided with Japan in the South China Sea and, only a few years later, the Chinese played silly games again – this time with the Philippines being the counterparty.

Finally, as far as coalition power is concerned, there appears to be a growing perception in the West that perhaps we shouldn't rely on our traditional coalition partners the way we have done for many years. Washington clearly doesn't rate the relationship with Europe as highly as it used to and, in Europe, ever since the Eurozone crisis blew up in 2011, the focus has been on keeping the Eurozone together rather than nurturing the relationship with the US.

More recently, the UK's decision to leave the EU hasn't exactly strengthened coalition powers in the West. Meanwhile, China has been very busy strengthening its own coalition powers – particularly in Africa, where it used to be non-existent. Consequently, it would only be fair to conclude that China's overall power is unquestionably rising and that, by association if for no other reason, the overall power of the East is rising.

China's likely impact on the rest of Asia

Over the past few centuries, several economic powerhouses have been launched. In the Industrial Revolution, England was the economic superpower and the driver of growth. Following World War I, the US took over and has since been the superpower of the world. I am struggling to see why China couldn't become the global superpower one day and thus have a massive effect on the rest of Asia.

As already pointed out, the very first consumer good that is positively affected by rising per capita income is food. Next comes housing – as people migrate to urban areas, housing is very much in demand. After housing comes transportation. I was in Vietnam a few years ago, and they are still at the scooter stage. After that comes the desire to own a car, and the next stage in the transportation cycle is when flying becomes the norm when travelling over longer distances.

The split between goods and services also changes quite dramatically as per capita income rises. In the very early stages, 100% of disposable income goes towards goods and nothing towards services, but that changes as people get more money in their hands. Based on the early experience from various emerging markets, the first service to be demanded by consumers are telephones – mostly mobile phones nowadays.

As per capita income rises, other sorts of services will increasingly be in demand – restaurants, take-away food, charter holidays and private schools to mention a few. The developed part of the world is still in this phase with services (as a % of GDP) continuing to rise year after year.

From an investment point of view, old world investors have the great advantage of having been through this entire cycle already. Unless Asians behave fundamentally differently from Europeans and North Americans (and why should they?) it should be straightforward to predict what happens next.

Finally, I should also point out that Asians in general are in awe of old world brands. The occasional queues outside the major retail stores in the West End of London are testament to that. This implies that, as per capita income rises across Asia, those queues will only get longer.

The flipside of the China story

Before I get too carried away and relinquish all power to the Chinese, let me make a couple of points. There is no doubt that China's economic power is growing: its risk tolerance is clearly higher than it is in the West; its threat power, if not higher today in absolute terms, is growing more rapidly; and its coalition power is also in ascendancy.

The China story is not quite so simple, though, as China's growth engine is extraordinarily one-dimensional. Investments account for nearly 50% of GDP, and its consumers continue to under-spend as general distrust in the government's welfare programme has driven savings rates to extreme levels.

Meanwhile, the country's investment programme is to a significant degree based on maintaining social stability, as millions of people continue to migrate from the rural parts of the country to urban areas in search of better times. As the urban population has swelled, the government has responded by creating jobs, often in construction, and habitually by building bridges to nowhere. This strategy has resulted in a banking industry that is over-leveraged and increasingly looking like an accident waiting to happen.

On top of that, China has never opened its current account, as it promised it would do when entering the WTO in December 2001. This has had the result of keeping the Chinese currency artificially low, providing an additional boost to Chinese GDP.

Had China opened its current account as it promised back in 2001, the renminbi would be dramatically higher than it is today, and annual GDP growth would probably be at least a couple of percentage points lower. Consequently, many believe the Chinese are simply cheating, and the rest of the world paying the price.

Could the West wake up one day and demand that China plays by the rules?

One of the problems is that the West is not unified in its criticism of China, weakening the coalition power. Being a major importer of Chinese goods, the US is in the hawks' camp (but have been lousy at bargaining), whereas Germany, being a net exporter to China, has taken a very different approach. Having said that, my guess is that, one day, the West will say that enough is enough.

Adding to that, there is most definitely a limit as to how much leverage the financial system can cope with, whether the Chinese are prepared to admit it or not. As we entered the new millennium, total debt-to-GDP in China was around 120%. As the Global Financial Crisis hit in 2008, debt-to-GDP was already over 200%, and now it is almost 350%, and many Chinese banks are in the danger zone.

One final point on China – it is not only when dealing with macroeconomic numbers that the Chinese cheat. Take the crisis in the South China Sea, where China first had a territorial dispute with Japan, and then one with the Philippines. Despite the international court in The Hague ruling against China, it chose to simply ignore that ruling.

That sort of behaviour clearly weakens China's coalition power, and could potentially turn the entire world against it. If they are not prepared to respect and adhere to international law, do you want to do business with them?

Investment implications

When doing an assessment of the investment implications of *the rise of the East*, one must make a general assumption on the health of the Chinese financial system.

Is it at risk of collapsing, or isn't it?

The Chinese have built a horrendous number of bridges to nowhere in recent years, and that is likely to come back and bite them at some point. You can extend and pretend for a while, and the Chinese can probably do so for longer than we would think possible, as the system is largely government controlled, but logic will ultimately prevail.

Consequently, I prefer to play this theme away from China. Invest in countries and investment strategies that benefit from rapid growth in China without being directly exposed to the Chinese financial system.

Firstly, aviation leasing in Asia. I note that this industry is not as cyclical as the underlying aviation industry is. Rising living standards throughout Asia in the years to come will put the growth rate of this industry at par with the growth we went through in mature economies back in the 1970s and 1980s, when flying became standard practice. Moreover, it is an investment strategy that generates a respectable amount of regular income. Fixed income investors should therefore treat the investment strategy as a proxy for corporate bonds.

Secondly, agriculture. As per capita income rises, the protein intake also rises. That has always been, and always will be, the case. As far as Asian consumers are concerned, if history were to repeat itself, meat will increasingly become part of the daily diet.

To supply more meat to billions of Asians, more beef, lamb and pork must be reared. Because of meat's limited shelf life and modest food budgets amongst Asian consumers, proximity and cost efficiency is important, and that is where Australia enters the frame. Australia can not only produce vast amounts of meat; they can also do it very cost effectively. Australia is therefore likely to be a major beneficiary of the overall Asian drive towards more protein-rich food.

Thirdly, trade finance, which is an investment strategy that provides export – and sometimes also import – finance, mostly to companies in emerging markets. Across Asia, not unlike Europe, banks have pulled away from much of this business in recent years, as they continue to repair their balance sheets in preparation for Basel III and IV[60]. The tightening of banking supervision rules is not likely to end any time soon, as regulators are keen to avoid another 2008. Expect more to come after Basel III and IV have been implemented.

An altogether different approach would be to invest in old world consumer brands, which appear to be in high demand in the East. Some would argue that old world property should also benefit from this trend, but I am not entirely convinced.

Growing nationalism in the UK, US and other countries could possibly lead to a ban on foreigners buying property, which would obviously hurt property prices in metropoles like London. I accept the risk of this happening is quite low, but I prefer to be on the safe side. Consequently, I would stay clear of that opportunity for now. Famous brands that Chinese visitors to London are prepared to join half a mile-long queues for are more my cup of tea.

---

60   Basel IV is effectively the full implementation of Basel III.

7

The Death of Fossil Fuels

Fossil fuels have been the key driver of economic growth since the Industrial Revolution. In this chapter, I argue that fossil fuels have come to the end of the road, and that the introduction of a new and much cheaper energy form is the key to get the economy going again.

Why fossil fuels will cease to exist

THE DEATH OF fossil fuels? A headline of that nature implies that I believe oil, gas and coal prices are heading towards $0. Do I really believe that? In the (very) long term, yes, at least as far as coal and gas prices are concerned. Almost all coal and gas is used either as a source of motive power (in power plants or elsewhere), in transportation, or to heat our homes, and that will all change in the years to come, but more about that below.

Oil is a little (but not much) different. In the US, 70–75% of all oil consumption goes towards transportation and only a modest amount goes towards the other two big end-users of oil – private homes (for heating) and the chemical industry (mostly to produce plastic products). Only the chemical industry will be largely unaffected by new energy forms. Oil will therefore not become obsolete any time soon but, 20–30 years from now, it could trade at a fraction of current levels.

The logic behind all of this is relatively straightforward. Fossil fuels tie up an increasing amount of capital stock. There is only a finite amount of capital available globally. When fossil fuel-producing countries require more capital to deliver the energy the world so desperately needs, it affects productivity *globally*. In that context, I note that, in the US, it requires 31 times more capital stock to extract a barrel of oil today than it did in 1977[61], just before everything started to decline.

The conventional way to evaluate fossil fuels

When I worked at Goldman Sachs back in the 1990s, I learned that fossil fuels are an integral part of American culture, much more than they are in Europe, even if the sector is very well represented in European equity indices. I also learned that the bulls and bears take a relatively simple approach – or at least they did back then.

Take oil. Oil-bears would typically build their case around the ongoing oversupply of oil (if there was one, and there usually was), which could be estimated on the back of how much oil was stored every day around the world. That number would then be assessed in the context of total daily consumption, which at present is around 95 million barrels. The bears would then look at excess storage capacity and, if that number was low, they would have a case.

The bulls would counter with an equally simple argument: "Oil prices have never traded below the marginal cost of production[62] for long" they would argue, and they were – and still are – broadly correct. Oil producers have always made cuts in output if (when) oil prices stay below marginal production costs for an extended period of time.

Other dynamics would obviously have an impact as well.

---

61   Source: The MacroStrategy Partnership (2017,1).
62   The marginal cost of production is often defined as the cost of increasing production by 1%. Example: If total oil production is around 95 mbd (as it is), the marginal cost of production is the cost of raising the daily production level by (just under) 1 mbd.

Take Saudi Arabia. They used to defend the price at all cost but, more recently, they have put more emphasis on protecting their market share. Unlike virtually any other oil-producing nation, the Saudis would still make a profit at $20 and have, consequently, chosen to defend their market share rather than the price. Such changes in tactics would obviously need to be built into the assessment.

The fiscal breakeven is another variable that affects the behaviour of oil-producing nations. As most oil-producing countries are very dependent on the income from oil to balance their books, they behave very differently, subject to what oil price they need for their books to balance.

Exhibit 7.1: Fiscal 2017 breakeven oil prices in various oil-producing countries (USD)

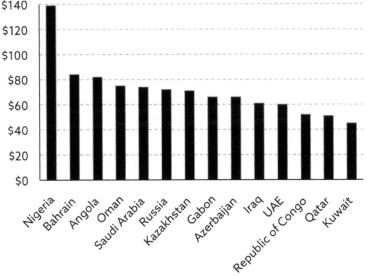

Source: Fitch Ratings (2017).

With Brent crude oil prices having averaged $54 in 2017, of all the major oil-producing nations[63], only Kuwait is likely to have produced a meaningful budget surplus in 2017. Some countries are very much in the red, with Nigeria requiring an oil price of almost $140 per barrel to balance its books (exhibit 7.1). Even worse, if one were to include countries not included in the Fitch survey, Libya, Venezuela and Yemen would all stand out, as all three countries have fiscal breakevens even higher than that of Nigeria.

Global energy production – before and after the emergence of shale

Global primary energy production has grown from 487 million tons of oil equivalents (mtoe) in 1900 to about 13,000 mtoe in 2016, leading to an annualised growth rate of nearly 3%. Behind that number hide some significant variations, though. The growth in energy production peaked in the 1950s and 1960s and has been slowing ever since (exhibit 7.2).

Earlier in this book, I credited President Eisenhower with what I called the transport revolution, and the need for energy certainly rose as more highways were built, and more people began to fly, but something else happened as well.

A post-World War II drive away from using coal as a direct source of motive power towards using it indirectly via electricity also boosted productivity – and hence GDP growth – in the 1950s and 1960s[64]. In the decades that followed, global energy production continued to increase as the economy expanded, but at a slowing pace.

Despite the sharp ramp-up in oil production from shale reserves, in the seven years from 2010 to 2016, the annual increase in energy production was only 1.3% – the slowest pace since 1900. Moreover, the effect shale has had on overall growth in energy production has been surprisingly modest.

---

[63]   Ex. Norway.
[64]   Source: The MacroStrategy Partnership (2017,3).

Exhibit 7.2: Annual energy production (mtoe) growth by decade and the seven years 2010-16

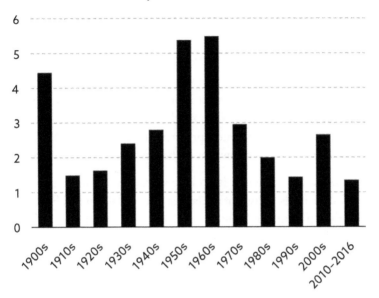

Source: The MacroStrategy Partnership LLP (2017,1).

Shale (both oil and gas) accounts for 25.2% of the increase in energy production between 2010 and 2016. If one were to exclude that, the 1.3% annualised growth rate would only drop to about 1%, so shale's importance shouldn't be exaggerated. I would certainly have expected shale to have made a more significant contribution to the growth in energy production in recent years.

Does shale production have a future?

US shale oil production peaked in March 2015. While nearly everybody has blamed the subsequent decline on relatively low oil prices, there is another way to think about it.

As productivity growth has flattened, so has GDP growth.

The combination of low (or no) GDP growth and high (and rising) energy production costs has resulted in energy prices that are still punitively high as far as economic growth is concerned. High oil inventory levels around the world is a testament to that logic.

The US economy has clearly benefitted from having a handful of shale oil and gas fields that have proven very productive. However, once you move away from those 5–6 sweet spots, productivity in the US shale industry drops immensely. Not a single shale field has been identified in the last couple of years, where productivity isn't at least 30% – and in some cases up to 90% – below that of the top shale fields in the country.

I also note that production is no longer accelerating in several of the top US shale fields. In two of the largest ones – Bakken and Eagle Ford – growth in production began to decelerate a couple of years before oil prices collapsed in 2014. With oil prices being well over $100 when the growth rate began to decelerate, you would have thought other reasons to be behind the slowdown – not oil prices.

When shale first emerged as a serious contender, typical production costs were in the $80s, but they have since dropped quite dramatically. The top US shale fields are now cash flow positive when oil prices are in the low $50s, and that obviously makes the industry a more serious contender at prevailing oil prices.

However, I also note that smaller US shale fields, as well as shale fields outside the US, need much higher oil prices to prevail. At present, even the most productive non-US fields need at least $65 to break even on a cash basis – and much higher prices to break even on a total cost basis. That can obviously change over time, but the appetite to invest in shale outside the US may be limited in the short term because of those economics.

The only conclusion I can reach is that shale production won't grow as much as (nearly) everyone expects and, consequently, it won't necessarily provide the 100% rainproof ceiling on oil prices that is the widely perceived result of the fracking technique. I don't expect shale to go away anytime soon, but neither do I expect it to become more than a modest factor in determining the overall balance between the global supply of, and demand for, fossil fuels.

The conventional conclusion

With shale likely to only play a modest role, the world will almost certainly be dependent on conventional fossil fuels for quite a while yet. In that context, I note that the global oil industry hasn't exactly prospered in terms of replacing all those older oil fields that are in decline. New finds are at the lowest point since World War II, and consumption has exceeded discoveries every year since the early 1990s (exhibit 7.3).

Exhibit 7.3: Global discoveries vs. global consumption (billion barrels)

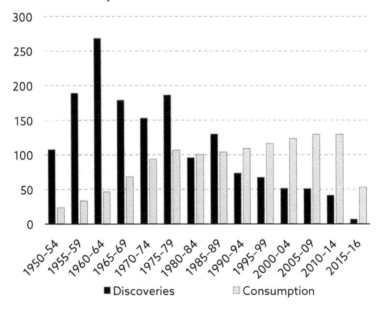

Source: Colin Campbell, IEA (2017).

Note: Barrels of conventional liquids. Excludes extra heavy oil and natural gas liquids.

In the past, once production in an oil field peaked, the annual rate of decline was on average 5–6%. New and better drilling techniques (e.g. horizontal drilling) have reduced the rate of decline in more recent years, though, and today it is not unusual for the rate of decline to be only a couple of percentage points post-peak.

The flipside of that is that the rate of decline will be much more sudden, when the oil field nears the end of its life. In that context, I note that, for many years, productivity in the oil industry benefitted from a shift to horizontal drilling; however, as that technique now dominates, the gains in productivity are much more limited.

Without the optimism generated by rising productivity, it is quite likely that investors at some point will lose the appetite for funding an industry with negative cash flows, such as the US shale industry. If you combine that with the knowledge that new oil finds are at an 80-year low, it is not at all impossible that depletion rates suddenly rise dramatically.

As a consequence of this, it is indeed quite tempting to paint a very dark picture. With shale unlikely to be the knight on the white horse many believe it is, a growing gap between consumption and new discoveries can hardly result in anything but energy prices that are high relative to the level of underlying economic growth. Higher energy prices act as a tax on consumers, so the net result will be even lower economic growth, and it is not inconceivable that growth will turn negative at some point.

The exergy model – an alternative way to determine the price of energy

There is a fundamentally different way to evaluate the price we pay for energy, and how that affects economic growth. In the following few paragraphs, I focus on oil, simply because the statistical output on oil is so much better than it is on coal and natural gas, but my conclusion would be no different on other fossil fuels.

It all begins with productivity growth in oil-producing countries, which has been in decline in recent years. You will see from exhibit 7.4 that almost all oil-producing nations have experienced negative growth in total factor productivity (TFP) in the last few years.

Exhibit 7.4: TFP in 15 largest oil-producing countries, 2012-16

	2012	2013	2014	2015	2016
Russia	1.7	0.0	−0.6	−4.0	−0.6
Saudi Arabia	−3.3	−5.5	−4.6	−2.6	−3.4
United States	0.1	-0.2	0.1	0.2	-0.3
Iraq	10.8	3.8	−2.5	1.5	6.1
Iran	1.2	1.0	1.6	1.4	1.5
Canada	−1.2	0.3	0.9	−0.9	0.0
UAE	1.3	−0.3	−1.5	−1.0	−0.6
Kuwait	1.3	−5.3	-6.3	-4.3	−3.6
Brazil	−1.8	−1.5	-2.6	-5.4	−3.6
Venezuela	2.3	−1.4	−6.4	-6.3	−16.9
Mexico	0.2	-1.5	0.5	-0.7	−0.8
Nigeria	3.1	1.8	1.9	-2.7	−6.8
Angola	0.8	1.5	-0.8	2.1	−1.2
Norway	−0.2	−1.5	−0.7	−0.1	−0.5
Kazakhstan	−1.5	1.2	0.7	−3.2	−1.8

Source: The Conference Board (2017).

TFP growth was extraordinarily negative during the height of the Global Financial Crisis, but it then recovered, only to turn negative again around 2013–14. As of early 2018, it remains extraordinarily negative.

I included 15 of the 16 largest oil-producing nations in exhibit 7.4. Only China has been excluded, as I don't fully trust the data coming out of Beijing. Even a quick look at the chart makes one realise that negative productivity growth in oil-producing nations is fast becoming a global issue.

As I said in the opening paragraphs of this chapter, deteriorating productivity in oil-producing countries leads to more capital stock tied up for every barrel of oil produced, which again leads to lower GDP growth – not only in oil-producing countries but everywhere. It all links back to the fact that the global capital pool available for productivity enhancing purposes is finite.

As per the exergy model (more on this below), GDP simply *cannot* grow at a reasonable rate without access to energy at a reasonable cost. It is a vicious circle that you don't easily escape from. Higher and higher exploration and production costs lead to lower and lower GDP growth. Unless we can find a new energy form that can be produced at a reasonable cost, the ultimate outcome of all of this is most likely negative GDP growth.

Furthermore, if you zoom in on the (few) positive numbers in exhibit 7.4, the story isn't as solid as it looks like at first glance. Take Iraq, which has posted solid TFP growth in most years since the new millennium; however, Iraq is still down from the levels posted before the first Gulf War in 1990. In 1991, Iraq's TFP collapsed – it was down 92.4%!

Given recent years' TFP statistics from most oil-producing nations, one can only wonder why oil production hasn't actually fallen. This question has simmered in the back of my head for many months, and the only answer I have been able to come up with is that oil production is only holding up because of various austerity programmes, and because the price of oil is still quite high in local currency terms.

Cutting public spending, selling FX reserves, devaluing the local currency, and hence devaluing real wages in the local oil industry, are all techniques that have been used around the world more recently to sustain energy output in an environment that doesn't justify for energy output to be sustained.

More on the exergy model

The thinking behind the exergy model is that falling productivity leads to falling energy production, and that again leads to falling output (GDP) – not just in oil-producing countries but *everywhere*.

As per the exergy model, you add up *all* energy production – and that would include food. You then measure the efficiency of converting that energy into productive work. I should point out that, although the exergy approach is very different from the conventional approach, you end up with the same GDP number, whichever approach you take.

The exergy model was introduced to me a while ago by Andrew Lees from the MacroStrategy Partnership LLP[65]. Exergy is a thermodynamic concept, conceived by engineers decades ago. It is defined as the maximum useful work which can be extracted from a system as it reversibly comes into equilibrium with its environment[66], and was developed as the shortcomings of existing models were increasingly being recognised.

In other words, it is the capacity of energy to do physical work or, as Andrew Lees puts it, it is the thermodynamic efficiency with which energy is converted into useful work. Instead of explaining GDP as a function of labour, capital and productivity, as we do when calculating GDP the conventional way, the exergy approach explains GDP as a function of labour, capital and exergy. Think of exergy as productivity.

It is not as far-fetched as it sounds. In nature, many things follow the same logistics curve as the exergy model does, and the reason is simple – it is all about thermodynamics. For any reader with an appetite for mathematics, GDP is defined the following way in the exergy model:

65 See www.macrostrategy.co.uk.
66 Source: Exergy Economics (2017).

Exhibit 7.5: The definition of GDP as per the exergy model

$$y = q \times u \; exp \left\{ f - a \left(\frac{u+l}{k-\delta} \right) + ab \frac{l}{u} + c \frac{\delta}{l} \right\}$$

$y = GDP$

$u = useful\ work$

$l = labour$

$k = capital\ stocks\ (total)$

$d = ICT\ capital\ stocks$

$[q, f, a, b, c] = fitting\ parameters$

Source: Exergy Economics (2017).

Which approach should you take?

Interestingly, the two different approaches to evaluate energy and its impact on economic growth arrive at pretty much the same conclusion, but the roads they take to get to that conclusion are very different indeed. The conclusion first: economic growth will, in the years to come, be lower than anything we have seen in the last 35–40 years – possibly even negative. That said, how do I reach that conclusion?

The conventional approach first. Because the oil industry is doing a very poor job in terms of replacing existing production (as we have just seen), the depletion rate[67] is rising and, in some countries, rather fast. This will eventually lead to a serious shortage of oil that will drive oil prices much higher.

However, higher oil prices will only have a limited effect on demand, as demand for oil is very inelastic. We still need to heat our homes,

---

67 Defined as annual production divided by proven reserves in producing oil fields.

etc. Higher oil prices are instead a tax on consumer spending, and the net result is therefore falling, eventually even negative, GDP growth.

The exergy approach next. As I have already said, those who have converted to the exergy model arrive at pretty much the same conclusion, even if they take a very different route. As per the exergy model, falling productivity leads to falling energy production, which again leads to shrinking GDP growth. Remember what I said earlier – exergy is just another word for productivity.

I am intrigued by the exergy model which makes a great deal of sense. Only time can tell whether thermodynamic principles can also be applied to economics, but the thought intrigues me. One could argue that it doesn't make much difference whether you subscribe to one model or the other. The result is the same. True, but also very handy when dealing with a new concept!

Why the death of fossil fuels?

Back to the opening statement of this chapter – the death of fossil fuels.

Why do I think that is a consequence of the above?

As I have stated frequently already, workforce growth and productivity growth are the two most fundamental drivers of GDP growth. With the outlook for workforce growth being rather pedestrian for many years to come, the only way GDP can grow at a reasonable rate is through superior productivity growth.

As we desperately need the economy to grow – otherwise we will literally drown in debt – we need to find ways to accelerate productivity growth, and one obvious way forward would be the introduction of a new and cheaper energy form. The consensus at present seems to be that solar energy is going to offer the solution we need, but I am not convinced.

Solar energy may address other problems, such as global warming, but it is very unlikely to fix our productivity problem. To be commercially viable, solar energy is still *very* dependent on subsidies and, although that might change over time, there is another and far cheaper alternative to solar energy.

The ultimate solution is fusion energy. Nothing would have a bigger impact on productivity growth than virtually unlimited access to cheap energy, and that is precisely what fusion energy brings to the table.

Instead of separating nuclear particles, as you do in nuclear power plants today (a technology called fission), you make nuclear particles collide, and that technology is called fusion.

I go into much more detail on fusion energy in chapter 10 – suffice to say for now that fossil fuels would become largely obsolete in a world powered by fusion energy – except for the modest amount of oil required by the chemical industry that I referred to earlier.

Investment implications

First and foremost, low productivity growth leads to low GDP growth, which again leads to low growth in corporate profitability. An obvious implication of that, combined with my findings in this chapter, is that investors should limit their beta exposure. Much more about that in chapter 12 – all I wish to say now is that taking broad market risk is not likely to be particularly rewarding in an environment of energy producing countries "confiscating" an ever larger share of the capital available.

The ultimate result, as I said earlier, is likely to be the introduction of a new energy form, which could completely transform the current low productivity environment into a high productivity environment. Could it be solar energy? Assuming it becomes cheaper over time, never say never, but solar energy is not even close to fusion energy in terms of where it is on the cost curve.

Having said that, the road we must negotiate to get to where we want, and how long that could take, is anything but certain. Fossil fuel prices could (and probably will) be all over the place before they ultimately go into hibernation. For that reason, a long-only strategy on fossil fuels could be akin to scoring a massive own goal.

8

Mean Reversion of Wealth-to-GDP

If US wealth-to-GDP has averaged about 3.8 over the decades (and probably centuries), and it is now 4.9, it goes without saying that something must give. That said, what is the logic behind wealth-to-GDP being long-term stable, and what are the implications, should we revert to the long-term mean value?

The background

Now to a trend that is perhaps not so easy to understand intuitively. Certain ratios have well established mean values, and the long-term mean value for US household wealth-to-GDP[68] is about 3.8 times[69]. In other words, if wealth-to-GDP is much different (as it is now), it will probably revert to the mean over time.

---

68 In this chapter, whenever I refer to household wealth or just wealth, I refer to the sum of household wealth and wealth controlled by non-profit organisations, which is how the Federal Reserve defines and measures US household wealth.
69 The same approach can be applied to P/E ratios, and the mean value for the US equity market P/E ratio is about 15.

In 1981, as we entered the Great Bull Market, total household wealth in the US stood at $11.5 trillion. Then the Great Bull Market took over, which resulted in extraordinary gains in wealth. So much wealth was created in the Great Bull Market of 1982–2000 that the wealth-to-GDP ratio in the US hit 4.8 at the turn of the century. It is a significant part of that increase in wealth that would have to have been given up, if the ratio were to mean revert.

And that is precisely what happened. The equity bear market of 2001–02 took the wealth-to-GDP ratio back to 3.6, and many expected that to be only the beginning of much worse to come. What those investors and commentators didn't anticipate was the impact the Greenspan Put[70] would have on risk taking and asset prices. Consequently, before the Global Financial Crisis decimated private wealth in 2007–09, the US wealth-to-GDP ratio went back up to a lofty 4.7 times.

Total US household wealth now stands at $96.9 trillion[71]. That is up from $11.5 trillion in 1981, just before the Great Bull Market took off. This has led to annual gains in aggregate household wealth of more than 6% – by far the strongest growth rate in wealth in all the years those numbers have been published by the Federal Reserve[72]. The $96.9 trillion of wealth should be looked at in the context of about $19.7 trillion of US GDP in 2017 (as of the end of 2017). In other words, US wealth-to-GDP is now a whopping 4.9 times.

To understand the deeper meaning of that number, think of wealth as capital and GDP as output. The wealth-to-GDP ratio is therefore the capital-to-output ratio, and an average ratio of 3.8 implies that it would (on average) take $3.8 of capital to produce $1 of output. Hence, the ratio is effectively a capital efficiency ratio, and the lower the ratio is, the more efficiently a country utilises the capital at its disposal.

---

[70] The Greenspan Put is a term used to describe the Federal Reserve's perceived desire under Alan Greenspan's leadership to prop up financial securities markets by lowering interest rates.

[71] As of the end of Q3 2017, according to the Federal Reserve.

[72] I have data going back to the early 1950s.

The fact that the growth of wealth continues to outpace the growth of GDP, and hence that the wealth-to-GDP ratio continues to rise, therefore implies that Americans utilise the capital at their disposal less and less efficiently. I also note that the US enjoys one of the lowest long-term mean values in the world, meaning that, in the past, the Americans have utilised capital more efficiently than we have done here in Europe, where the long-term mean value of wealth-to-GDP is 4.7 by comparison.

A fall in wealth-to-GDP from 4.9 to 3.8 times would likely result in vast losses of wealth. The last time the Americans experienced a significant and sustained loss of wealth was during the 1966–81 secular bear market, where wealth fell by over 3% per annum.

A full retreat to the long-term mean of 3.8 times would imply a decline in US household wealth of about $22 trillion (assuming GDP is largely unchanged), so it is not exactly pocket money we are talking about. I note that total net worth in the US troughed at $56 trillion in December 2008 at the bottom of the Global Financial Crisis, $41 trillion below current net worth. In that context, a loss of $22 trillion of household wealth doesn't look absurd.

The link to economic growth theory

As I pointed out in chapter 5, capital's share of national income has been stable over the decades and even centuries[73], and now I am arguing that wealth-to-GDP is also long-term stable.

Is there any link between the two?

You need to go back to economic growth theory, which is admittedly a rather heavy subject. According to the theory, regardless of how developed the underlying economy is, the capital-to-output ratio is

---

73   Data for the UK going back to 1850 suggests that the ratio between labour and income has been largely stable for at least 165 years. See Gollin (2002).

largely constant. Depending on how capital is defined[74], it takes about four units of capital to generate one unit of output.

As I have just pointed out, the mean value of wealth-to-GDP (capital-to-output) in the US over the very long term is about 3.8 times. Now, if you think of national income as a proxy for output and output as GDP, it is suddenly logical why both capital's share of national income and wealth-to-GDP is long-term stable.

In other words, it all makes perfect sense, unless there is something fundamentally wrong with economic growth theory, but that is not the subject of this book. I will simply assume that the theory is correct. At least those economists, who have developed the theory, have the empirical evidence firmly on their side.

There is another way to think of all of this. If the amount of capital relative to output is above average, as it is at present, then the return on that capital will be lower, as the excess amount of capital raises the overall level of competition. Consequently, people save less, and that reduces the amount of capital over time. Hence the capital-to-output ratio drops, and so does wealth-to-GDP.

The road to mean reversion

As the full impact of the Global Financial Crisis became apparent, nobody was surprised to see that the wealth-to-GDP ratio had dropped back towards its long-term mean value. In the US, it landed at about 3.6 times. Greenspan had retired by then, but the Greenspan Put was still alive and kicking; now in the form of QE, and wealth-to-GDP began to climb yet again.

In the context of the ongoing rise in US wealth-to-GDP, I note that US wages have begun to rise again when measured as a percentage of GDP, following a slump that lasted almost 15 years, and that has caused a squeeze on corporate profits. It is still early days, but such a change will obviously affect the capital-to-output ratio and, in the national

---

74   In early growth models, human capital was not included. It is now.

accounts, it will affect the share of national income that goes to labour; hence it will also affect wealth-to-GDP. Perhaps the long-awaited mean reversion has already begun?

If economic laws haven't changed – and I am yet to hear a single solid argument in favour of that – then, sooner or later, the Americans will head back to a wealth-to-GDP ratio of about 3.8[75]. Now that can happen in two different ways. Either private wealth drops significantly, or the numerator (wealth) grows more slowly than the denominator (GDP) over a longer period of time.

Should equilibrium be re-established simply by wealth growing more slowly than GDP for a longer period of time, given that GDP won't grow particularly fast for many years to come, financial asset prices could move virtually sideways for a painfully long time.

When is all this likely to happen?

Assuming the wealth-to-GDP ratio is indeed stable, the obvious follow-up question to ask is *when* will the ratio mean revert? There is not much point in knowing that wealth-to-GDP will drop at some point, if it won't happen in our lifetime. This is, however, not so simple; there is no mathematical solution to that question. That said, if one understands the circumstances that have driven wealth-to-GDP to 4.9 times, one can arrive at some conclusions.

When you plot the ratio over the last 100 years, no single set of data explains much of the variation. In other words, no single factor explains why wealth-to-GDP is so high at present. In many ways, it would be much simpler if one factor could explain all the variation, but that is not the case. A combination of factors appears to be at work.

In chapter 10, I will assess whether there is anything on the horizon, which could fundamentally alter the rather bleak world I see in front of us. One such possible saviour is automation. Robots are increasingly

---

75 The decline in wealth-to-GDP will probably even over-shoot temporarily to drive the long-term mean value down to 3.8 times.

being used on manufacturing floors around the world, but it is only the beginning, and it won't be long before robots are used in the financial industry as well. Given the track record of many active investment managers, I am sure we will see one or two being replaced by robots before long, but more about that in chapter 10.

As automation intensifies in the years to come, the need for capital will continue to rise, but the very high capital-to-output ratio that we currently enjoy suggests to me that the capital needed is there. When the history books about the post-crisis environment eventually are written, it wouldn't surprise me if automation will be assigned a leading role, when economists seek to explain the concept of mean reversion.

When I first tuned into this topic, I thought wealth-to-GDP was high mainly because of low interest rates, but could it be the other way round? Could it be that interest rates are not (only) low because of QE, but (also) because the world is awash in capital? It certainly looks like it, even if almost the entire world tends to think that QE is what has driven interest rates lower.

A critique of the underlying theory

The underlying theory that wealth-to-GDP *must* mean revert is based on empirical evidence. Yes, it is an important part of economic growth theory and, yes, the anecdotal evidence in place very much supports that theory, but I cannot present a mathematical proof that the ratio is *always* long-term stable, because no such proof exists.

The stable nature of wealth-to-GDP was first recognised by the Swedish economist Knut Wicksell, and he used it in much of his work in the late 19th century. In mathematical terms, the stable nature of the capital-to-output ratio was first expressed by Paul Douglas (economist) and Charles Cobb (mathematician). Their work in the 1920s turned into what is now known as the Cobb-Douglas production function. The standard version of that production function with only two input factors – capital (K) and labour (L) – states that output (Y) can be defined as follows:

$$Y = AK^{\alpha}L^{1-\alpha}$$

Where:

A = Total factor productivity

α = Output elasticity of capital ($0 < \alpha < 1$)

In economics, the Cobb–Douglas production function is a functional form of the production function, used to represent the technological relationship between the amounts of two or more input factors – usually capital and labour as above – and the amount of output that can be produced by those inputs. If the relationship between capital and output is stable, the production function is said to be a Cobb-Douglas function.

As I stated earlier, if wealth-to-GDP has been (largely) stable for as long as we have measured it, but is now well above its long-term mean value (as it is), the capital-to-output ratio cannot be stable as the Cobb-Douglas production function prescribes. Something must be astray.

With central banks playing games with the free market forces through QE, one could argue that what has worked in the past, may not necessarily work so well at present. However, as we also know, free market forces will ultimately prevail. The Bank of England recognised as much when, back in 2011, it acknowledged that the public should prepare for more difficult times post-QE[76].

Another possible explanation is that other input factors have upset the stable relationship between capital, labour and output. In chapter 6 I introduced the concept of incentive structures. They are a mishmash of different input factors – all non-quantifiable. The quality of the education system is one such factor, but the most important of them all is probably government regulation.

Could one or more of these factors have changed the economic landscape so fundamentally that the capital-to-output ratio is no longer stable? I guess everything is possible, but I am yet to hear a convincing

---

76   Source: Bank of England (2011).

reason why that should be the case. And the fact that we, not once but twice since the millennium, have seen wealth-to-GDP drop back to its long-term mean value tells me that the theory behind it still applies.

Investment implications

It is tempting to finish this chapter with a conclusion that the outlook is straightforward. Asset prices will simply fall across the board until equilibrium has been re-established. End of story. Such a simplistic approach would imply that those asset classes that have risen the most in value will also fall the most, but things are not that simple.

Which distinctly British asset class do you think has offered the most attractive returns over the past decade? Central London property? Not even close, even if it has done rather well. UK farmland is the answer, having more than tripled in value over the last decade which will otherwise not be remembered for its outsized returns.

The simplistic approach referred to above would therefore imply that British farmland is the most exposed asset class there is. However, as I pointed out in chapter 6, *the rise of the East* will most likely lead to a massive increase globally in the demand for food products, which could benefit farmland prices in the UK.

As far as the US is concerned, the median family owns next to no bonds and only a limited amount of equities, so the only asset class that matters to them in terms of establishing how wealthy they are is the value of the family home. This picture varies from country to country but, at least as far as the UK is concerned, I wouldn't reach a dramatically dissimilar conclusion.

That doesn't at all imply that bonds and equities don't matter. Of course they do, but falling bond and equity prices will only have a limited impact on the average American or British family, whereas falling property prices will do significant damage.

This becomes important in the context of how I expect those three asset classes to respond to my expected drive towards mean reversion of wealth-to-GDP.

I expect bond markets to perform relatively well in the years to come. Given the excessive amount of debt almost everywhere, central bankers realise there will be plenty of blood in the streets if interest rates were to normalise. They are therefore likely to use whatever tools they have at their disposal to keep interest rates relatively low.

Equities next. Going back to exhibit 2.1 for a minute, the numbers in that table can be presented in a different way. When doing that, it becomes obvious that we are at the high end of a channel that was first established about 150 years ago (exhibit 8.1).

Exhibit 8.1: S&P Composite, 1877 to present

Source: Advisor Perspectives (2017,1).

Note: Inflation-adjusted monthly averages of daily closes.

Now, I should point out that there are no rules as to how long secular bull or bear market should last for, but history provides some guidelines. Only one has run for more than 20 years, and neither any secular bull nor any secular bear market has *ever* breached the limits of the channel outlined in exhibit 8.1.

As you can see, the secular bull market we have been in since 2009 is dramatically above the long-term trend line but, when secular bear markets take charge, equity markets rarely just go back to the trend line. Most of them go all the way back to the bottom of the channel. In other words, there is considerable downside risk associated with holding equities – particularly US equities[77] – in the current environment.

I don't think equities will necessarily be the worst performing asset class, though. Property has enjoyed an extended period of good times, and it wouldn't surprise me at all, if the road to mean reversion starts with falling property prices. In the UK, a whole generation of property buyers (those aged 40 and younger) have never experienced falling property prices and don't think it can ever happen.

Let me finish this chapter with a tale from the office. A colleague of mine was house hunting in London a while ago. He found a flat he liked and put a bid in a good 10% below the asking price. The seller's reaction was worth a cartoon series. "You don't understand", he said. "I need the asking price, as I am buying another flat". My colleague felt tempted to say in a very apologetic tone: "Oh sorry. Why didn't you tell me? If you need that, of course I shall pay it. Anything else you need?". Wisely, he kept his mouth shut.

---

[77] Partly because US wealth-to-GDP is particularly high at present, partly because US equities are particularly expensively priced.

9

The Perfect Storm

I have now completed my evaluation of the six structural mega-trends that I have identified. Although they won't necessarily all be detrimental to economic growth going forward, some of them most definitely will. There is a risk – and it is not insignificant – that at least some of the six trends will combine and establish what could resemble the perfect storm. Investors are advised to take such a potential outcome into consideration, when constructing their portfolios.

The classic macroeconomic approach

THERE IS NOT just one or two but several different ways you can measure and evaluate GDP growth. So that we can make the appropriate comparisons, let's start from first principles and define GDP in a very orthodox, macroeconomic way.

The classic approach is straightforward. Across the economy, you add up all returns over the cost of capital, and the sum equals GDP. You may recall the formula I presented in chapter 3: GDP was divided into four chunks – consumer spending, corporate investments, government spending and net exports – and it came out as the sum of the four:

$$GDP = C + I + G + (X - M)$$

Just about every civilised country on planet Earth reports GDP this way. When I started to read economics back in the early 1980s, the equation above was one of the very first elements of economic wisdom I was introduced to, and it was presented to us still wet-behind-the-ears students as the holy grail.

In the low-growth environment I see in front of us, governments all over the world will increasingly look at public spending (G) and use it to accelerate GDP growth. That said, public spending is a host of different things. Some forms of public spending are known to have a very low multiplier, whereas others give the broader economy an instant kick.

Take transfer payments vs. infrastructure spending. The first will grow massively in the years to come due to the ageing of society but, sadly, it will have little impact on overall economic growth. In fact, the net effect is most likely going to be negative due to rising indebtedness, which will hold back productivity growth. By contrast, infrastructure spending is usually good for productivity, and should therefore be encouraged.

Since assuming office, Donald Trump and his cabinet have repeatedly used the figure of $1 trillion over 10 years to demonstrate the scale of their vision regarding US infrastructure spending, which has created a bit of a stir in financial markets. That is all good, but what looks like significant infrastructure spending is in fact dwarfed by the cost of rising transfer payments in the years to come (exhibit 9.1).

Exhibit 9.1: Trump's infrastructure programme vs. rising US benefit costs (USD billions)

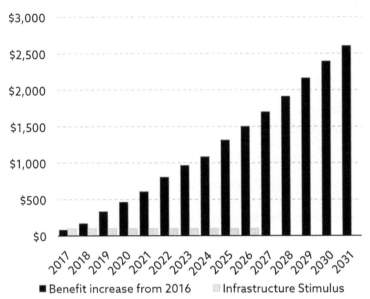

■ Benefit increase from 2016 ▨ Infrastructure Stimulus

Source: DanielAmerman.com (2017).

Note (1): Trump's $1 trillion infrastructure programme has been divided evenly over a 10-year period.

Note (2): Benefit costs include social security, Medicare and Medicaid.

The exergy approach

Another way to measure GDP is the so-called *exergy approach*, which I introduced in chapter 7. Assuming this is not a concept you have worked with before, let me recap what I said earlier. Exergy is the capacity of energy to do physical work. Think of exergy and productivity as one and the same thing.

In the world of exergy economics, we are very much on a slippery slope right now. Productivity growth has been declining for the last half century after peaking in the 1950s and 1960s and has turned outright negative in the last four years – globally that is.

The ultimate consequence of declining productivity is lower energy production and falling, possibly even negative, GDP growth. Those who subscribe to the exergy model believe it is a vicious circle that it is almost impossible to escape from.

The demographic approach

However, there is an altogether simpler approach of measuring GDP growth[78]. All the way back in chapter 1, I introduced a very simple model:

$$\Delta GDP = \Delta Workforce + \Delta Productivity$$

In other words, the change in economic output equals any change to the workforce plus any change in productivity. It is also my favourite approach when I estimate trend GDP growth. Just don't use this methodology to measure GDP growth from one year to the next.

The change in productivity (ΔProductivity) is a residual factor, calculated as the change in GDP less the change in the workforce. ΔProductivity is therefore a mishmash of all the components that affect GDP growth except for changes to the workforce – factors as diverse as labour productivity, the efficiency of capital and land, government regulations, new technology, etc. Over a full economic cycle (or longer), the equation works very well, though; hence it is a superb indicator of trend growth.

The microeconomic approach

As I got further into my studies at university, microeconomics entered the frame, and I was advised to forget about my newly acquired macroeconomic wisdom for a while. My professor told me to look at the economy from a bottom-up point of view instead.

---

[78]   You can only apply this method when estimating the change in GDP; not the absolute level thereof.

Assume there are n companies in the private sector, and think of private sector GDP as the sum of the value-added created by those n companies. The value-added is defined as total revenues created by the n companies (R) less the cost of generating those revenues (C):

$$GDP_{\text{Private Sector}} = \Sigma(R_n - C_n)$$

All you would have to do to arrive at the same number for GDP as in the classic macroeconomic model, would be to add government spending (G):

$$GDP = \Sigma(R_n - C_n) + G$$

Let's focus on the private sector for a minute. Under reasonable assumptions, $\Delta GDP_{\text{Private Sector}} = \Sigma\Delta R_n$ and $R = P \times Q$ (revenues equal price multiplied by quantity), i.e.:

$$\Delta GDP_{\text{Private Sector}} = \Sigma\Delta(P_n \times Q_n)$$

Extending the work I did back in chapter 5, it is worth noting that P and Q are a function of the S-curve and the D-curve in exhibit 5.1. Mathematically, a change in economic growth in the private sector can therefore be expressed as follows:

$$\Delta GDP_{\text{Private Sector}} = f(\Delta S_n, \Delta D_n)$$

The conclusion is obvious. The real reason the economy has ground to a near halt in recent years is that we have created an environment that has allowed supply to move out much faster than demand, and that we could accelerate economic growth again, if we could somehow find a way to accelerate aggregate demand over and above that of aggregate supply.

Explaining the stagnation in economic growth in this microeconomic way is relatively new thinking in economic circles and, if the theory is correct, addressing mediocre economic growth shall require a policy approach fundamentally different from the one applied in recent years (i.e. monetary policy).

How do the four different approaches compare?

By lining all these different GDP models up, am I saying that one is better than the others? Not really. That is not my point at all, although one could argue that they all have different strengths and weaknesses.

The classic macroeconomic approach benefits from its simplicity, and it is considered a valuable tool when economists (try to) explain to politicians which buttons to push. The exergy approach forces you to think differently in terms of how you create economic growth, which is why it is a very valuable tool. Consequently, it should gain traction in the years to come; however, it is far from simple, and will be almost impossible to explain to laypeople.

The demographic approach is brilliant as a secular forecasting tool and benefits immensely from its extraordinary simplicity, but should never be used for short-term forecasting purposes. The microeconomic approach is a relatively new approach in economic circles, and it remains to be seen if our political leadership will adapt to it.

Whether one is better than the others is not the purpose of bringing them all up in this context, though. My point is a different one. As I reviewed future expected GDP growth in the light of the four different GDP models, it became obvious to me that three of the four models imply one and the same thing. If we continue to sit on our hands and assume everything will return to normal, *GDP growth will eventually turn negative*. Simple as that.

The challenge is that the model used by nearly everyone – the classic model – doesn't imply anything of that sort; i.e. it will take a great deal of education of our political leaders, if they are to be convinced that the hole we are in will only get deeper, if we do nothing.

A quick recap of the six structural mega-trends

Before I go into a more in-depth discussion as to how the six structural mega-trends could interact, allow me to repeat the six trends that have been reviewed in this book:

1. The end of the debt super-cycle

2. The retirement of the baby boomers

3. The declining spending power of the middle classes

4. The rise of the East

5. The death of fossil fuels

6. Mean reversion of wealth-to-GDP

Of the six trends, the first three are outright negative for economic growth, and supposedly negative for equity returns as well. How each of them will affect interest rates is more of a mixed story, but more about that below.

The fourth trend (*the rise of the East*) is a mixed story. Much will depend on savings rates in China, which are extraordinarily high – mostly because the Chinese don't trust their own government to look after those in need. If that attitude were to change, the Chinese could establish a much better balance between the different sources of growth, and the Chinese economy could become exceptionally powerful.

Trend number five, *the death of fossil fuels*, could be quite negative for economic growth, at least in the short to medium term, but more about that below. Finally, the last trend – which is more a theme than a trend – could become the endgame of the Global Financial Crisis, just like World War II became the endgame of the last debt super-cycle.

So much has been said in recent years in terms of how it will all end. The most devastating economic calamity of the 20th century – the Great Depression – ended with Hitler and World War II, and it is more than a bit disconcerting that nationalism is on the march again, and this time mostly in the countries that fought Hitler less than a century ago. People never learn, do they?

If you go even further back in history, I would suggest that every major crisis throughout history has been associated with some sort of endgame, but it is never the same. Could my structural trend number 6 be the endgame of the Global Financial Crisis, which would imply significant downside risk to property?

A re-calibration of wealth-to-GDP ratios alone may not be enough to reset everything, but if it were to coincide with some other major calamity such as a significant sovereign default (Italy?), or a complete collapse of the DB pension system, it certainly could.

How the various structural trends could interact

As the first three trends are very interconnected, and as at least two of the three – the ageing consumer and his declining spending power – have had the impact of decimating GDP growth, authorities have been guilty of pursuing an extraordinarily easy monetary policy in a misunderstood attempt to solve all problems with only one policy tool.

Years ago, the Dutch economist Jan Tinbergen demonstrated that if policy makers want to address n problems, at least n policy tools shall be required. Why our leaders suddenly think they can fix everything with only one policy tool (monetary policy) is beyond me.

Anyway, what has been achieved with the extraordinary low interest rates of recent years is that savings-induced consumer spending has been converted to debt-induced consumer spending. This means that another of my trends – the end of the debt super-cycle – is very much part of the same story.

The extraordinarily low interest rates that we supposedly all benefit from form one of the biggest challenges Europe has faced since the war.

How I can possibly think of low interest rates as a challenge?

After all, don't we all benefit from exceedingly low mortgage rates, which pays for those extra couple of weeks in Mallorca every year? Life isn't that simple, though.

DB pension schemes are struggling to meet their obligations, and life insurance companies may go bankrupt *en masse,* if interest rates stay this low for much longer.

Why is that?

Because they are both subject to fixed future liabilities, the present value of which increases when interest rates fall. Given the dramatic fall in interest rates in recent years, future liabilities are suddenly much higher when discounted back to a present value.

That said, the most frightening problem of them all is that *people are angry.* They are very angry indeed, and when people are angry, you never know what happens next. The Anglo-Saxon habit of spending nearly every penny earned prevents the British and the Americans from fully appreciating this problem. That said, how do you think people in savings-based cultures such as the German-speaking part of Europe reacted when they discovered that they must now pay their bank a fee for the right to deposit their savings?

Why do you think parties like *Alternative für Deutschland* in Germany and *Front National* in France have blossomed in recent years? Because people are angry. In the simple (but not necessarily narrow-minded) world of the average man in the street, living standards are no longer rising. On top of stagnating living standards, if you also must pay your bank to look after your savings, no wonder anger is at the risk of boiling over.

Meanwhile, the elite assumes the mob is plain stupid, but it would be a monumental mistake to underestimate the mob, as King Louis XVI learned when the mob took control of his country during the French revolution. I am not anticipating a revolution like the one we had in France in the late 18th century, but less can also do great damage.

Utilising MacroStrategy's way to look at GDP growth through the exergy model, it becomes obvious why the fifth of the trends listed above (the death of fossil fuels) could also become a serious constraint on economic growth until we figure out a way to reduce the vast, and growing, amount of capital stock tied up in energy production.

The oil industry is doing a poor job in terms of replacing producing oil fields and has done so since the 1980s, when oil consumption for the first time exceeded oil discoveries. Global oil consumption runs at about 35 billion barrels per annum, whereas discoveries are now below 10 billion barrels annually[79]. This will have a major, and overwhelmingly negative, impact on GDP growth going forward.

The one exception – the rise of the East

Of the six structural trends, one could therefore argue that only one – *the rise of the East* – could possibly turn into a positive for economic growth. When I began to research the different trends in preparation for this book, I was actually inclined to call it *the rise of the East and the decline of the West*[80].

The rise of the East is indisputable – *the decline of the West* less so, though. The West will, in many ways, benefit from a rising East; however, with (i) a declining workforce, (ii) a growing population of elderly who will be tremendously expensive to service, (iii) a large part of the workforce who face declining living standards, (iv) a humongous mountain of debt that, instead of being used to enhance productivity, is increasingly used unproductively, and (v) rising energy exploration and production costs, I am struggling to be overly optimistic as far as the West is concerned.

That said, there will unquestionably be a significant positive impact on the West from rising living standards in the East, and I recommend long-term investors to structure their portfolio with that theme in mind.

---

79   Source: The MacroStrategy Partnership (2017,1).
80   I would include more mature economies such as Japan and Korea in my definition of the West.

A few thoughts on automation

You may recall that, in the introduction to this book, I touched on the subject of automation. Back in late 2015, BofAML released a monster of a research paper on the subject[81]. It certainly opened my eyes to the opportunity set laid out in front of us, but also to the potential damage a massive wave of advanced robotics can do to the employment market in the years to come.

BofAML's research analysts argued that robots will take over nearly 50% of all manufacturing jobs and shave $9 trillion off labour costs within a decade. I don't know enough about robots to argue for or against those numbers and the suggested timeline of it all, but the trend is clear, and the driver is first mover advantage.

As this is highly likely to happen concurrently with the other structural trends that are reviewed in this book, most of which will further slow economic growth, it is quite possible that history may not repeat itself. In the past, not one technological advance has led to rising unemployment. Yes, jobs have been lost, but other doors have opened.

This time could be different, though. So many jobs will be lost as a result of advanced robotics, and the economy may not be strong enough to create new opportunities for those affected. It is not a given, but it is certainly a risk and, should this time be different, the net effect of increased automation on economic growth may not be nearly as profound as (nearly) everybody expects. More on automation in chapter 10.

---

81   BofAML (2015).

10
How to Improve Productivity

As I began to prepare for this book, a little devil popped up inside my head, asking the same question again and again. Could anything possibly happen that would switch the lights back on again? This chapter is looking for answers to that question.

The problem in a nutshell (first take)

As I have repeatedly pointed out up to this point, GDP growth, both in nominal and in real terms, productivity growth as well as inflation have been trending down for many years – by most accounts since the 1970s. It is very convenient to blame it all on the Global Financial Crisis, but that one simply doesn't fly. After all, the Global Financial Crisis happened some 30 years after this downtrend was first formed. Something more fundamental must be astray.

It goes without saying that, if we want to reverse the downtrend, first and foremost, we need to understand why so much continues to trend in the wrong direction. You can argue that productivity, economic growth, inflation and interest rates are all part of the same story, so no wonder they are trending down at the same time, but that argument provides little insight into the underlying cause(s).

I return to the basic premises of this book:

1. The world is drowning in debt.

2. The workforce has begun to shrink, as the baby boomers retire in large numbers.

3. The middle classes no longer enjoy the rise in real wages they used to.

In other words, a combination of three undercurrents happens to be unfolding at the same time. Any one of those undercurrents would be enough to slow things down. No wonder there is not much growth anywhere, when all three undercurrents unfold concurrently.

Allow me to return to a formula I have introduced several times already:

$$\Delta GDP = \Delta Workforce + \Delta Productivity$$

The workforce has begun to shrink in most countries outside Africa so, to generate respectable economic growth, one would need for productivity to grow quite briskly, but it isn't – *anywhere.*

As I have already pointed out, productivity is a function of many factors and is measured in different ways, the most common one of which is labour productivity, but labour is far from the only factor having an impact on productivity.

Away from labour productivity, the incentive structure may be the most important of all the productivity factors. Behind that term lies everything government controls – the tax structure, rules and regulations, etc. Over the decades, it has become obvious that governments do more damage to productivity than anybody else, mostly by constantly introducing new rules and regulations.

I am not at all suggesting all rules and regulations are bad; they certainly aren't, but it is important that everyone, and particularly those in power, understands the negative impact rules and regulations can have on productivity and hence on economic growth.

With workforce growth being largely non-existent, and labour productivity growth in decline, as it has been globally since early this millennium (exhibit 10.1), one shouldn't be overly surprised that most countries are struggling to deliver any meaningful economic growth. Only those countries that grow their workforce at a reasonable rate continue to post solid GDP growth, and those countries are mostly African.

Exhibit 10.1: Trend growth of labour productivity, 1970–2017 (%)

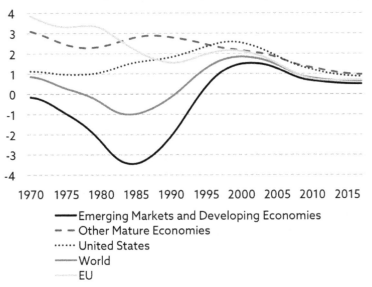

Emerging Markets and Developing Economies
— — Other Mature Economies
······ United States
——World
············EU

Source: The Conference Board (2017).

Note: Productivity measured as output per person.

Declining productivity growth affects *everything*. It obviously affects GDP growth, but it also affects energy prices, and it affects corporate profitability and hence companies' ability to service debt and their ability to increase wages.

One could argue that productivity is negatively impacted by ageing, as older people are less productive than the younger generations are, and that is true.

One could also argue that excessive debt levels affect productivity negatively, as capital that could otherwise be used productively is instead used to service existing debt.

A simple way to measure the magnitude of that problem is to look at how much GDP grows for every additional dollar of debt you assume. Years ago, before the world fell in love with debt, it was quite normal for GDP to grow in line with the growth in debt.

Not anymore.

The most indebted countries are down to $0.20 of GDP growth for every dollar of additional debt. It therefore doesn't seem unreasonable to suggest that up towards 80% of new capital (debt) is misallocated in the most indebted countries.

Consequently, I conclude that ageing and vast amounts of misallocated capital appear to be the two most important underlying reasons why productivity growth is in decline. However, that answer provides few solutions. Let me therefore ask again. Is there *anything* we could do to increase productivity despite poor demographics and despite drowning in debt?

Demographics

Immigration

Let's begin by taking a closer look at various demographic factors – immigration first. As Mrs Merkel in Germany has clearly understood, but perhaps not communicated as well as she could – and should – have, one obvious way to address the ageing problem is to allow more refugees into your country.

She allowed hundreds of thousands of refugees from Syria to settle in Germany, before any other European country got its act together. By being early, Germany benefitted from the fact that a significant proportion of the early Syrian settlers were well-educated people.

Sadly, Germany also ended up with a few youngsters who couldn't distinguish between right and wrong, and the country paid a very high price for that. Regrettably, that has coloured the public's view on immigration all over Europe, and there is absolutely no chance that *any* European country will follow Germany's lead any time soon.

Female participation in the workforce

Quite often I hear even well-informed people suggest that all we need to do for the ageing problem to go away is to increase the female participation in the workforce. There is only one problem with that argument. The numbers don't stack up.

According to the UN, which provides regular updates on female-to-male participation rates in the global workforce[82], female participation began to gather momentum in developed countries in the 1980s, and the trend continues to this day.

The countries with the highest female participation have a female-to-male participation ratio around 90 today, and UN data from recent years suggest that, when the ratio reaches that level, it begins to flatten out, i.e. one shouldn't expect it to increase much more than that[83].

The one country standing out is Japan, where the female-to-male ratio is still below 70. However, a closer examination of that number reveals that it is only amongst the over 40-year olds that female participation is low. Female participation amongst younger Japanese women is in line with other mature economies.

It is therefore only fair to conclude that Japan probably won't experience the boost in workforce growth from increased female participation that many expect, and that higher female participation in general is a drop in

---

[82] Defined by the UN as the ratio of female to male proportion of a country's working-age population that engages in the labour market, either by working or actively looking for work, expressed as a percentage of the working-age population.

[83] Source: United Nations (2016).

the ocean in most developed countries when compared to the number of people who will retire from the workforce over the next few decades.

Retirement age

Tired after a long life in the fields, my grandfather needed his daily nap. One day he was particularly tired and informed my grandmother that he would have a quick snooze before lunch. He never woke up again. He was only 76.

People are not ready to check out that early these days. When I look at my parents (who are in the early 80s) and their friends, I can see that retirement today means something entirely different than it did to my grandfather. Hence it is not inconceivable that many could retire much later than they do today.

Think about it the following way. Years ago, when the prevalent pension model was first adopted, life expectancies for newly retired people were 8–10 years, and pension models were constructed accordingly. Life expectancies, from the day people retire, now exceed 20 years. No wonder so many pension plans are deeply underwater.

Having many pension plans with substantial funding deficits only causes the decline in productivity to deteriorate further, as capital that could otherwise be used productively is used to bail out retirees from underfunded pension schemes. Hence, if people were to retire later in life, not only would pension plans' funding deficit fall, but productivity would most likely improve.

In practice, I can think of two caveats, though. Firstly, governments will face massive resistance as they move forward with plans like these[84]. The prevailing view amongst people approaching retirement – and their unions – is that this is not their problem, and governments shouldn't touch what they have earned over a lifetime. There is little sympathy for, and no willingness to understand, the bigger picture amongst these

---

[84] The Danish government is pushing ahead with plans to change the mandatory retirement age and have run into massive resistance.

people. And political parties are reluctant to touch the subject, as it is most certainly not a vote winner.

Secondly, even with the best of intentions, older workers are not as productive as the younger ones are. Productivity peaks when people are 30–40 years of age. It then stays relatively flat over the next 10 years or so, following which it begins to decline. Extending work life may therefore not have as big an impact on overall productivity levels as one would expect. On the other hand, you would expect this issue to gradually fade away as physical demands on most jobs become less and less stringent.

Monetary policy

Ever since the back of inflation was broken with a spell of extraordinarily high interest rates in the late 1970s and early 1980s, inflation targeting has been at the centre of monetary policy, and 2% annual inflation has been deemed the desirable level – at least in more mature economies. With several structural trends continuing to drive inflation down, one could argue (and I do) that inflation targeting should be shelved – at least temporarily.

The combination of inflation targeting and structurally low inflation has had the effect of plenty of capital being misallocated every year – capital that could, and should, have been used productively, has instead been used unproductively. The best example of that is probably the vast amounts of capital that is finding its way into property at present.

As I stated earlier, upwards of 80% of all new capital is misallocated in the worst affected countries at present. Capital that is misallocated (i.e. used unproductively) not only has the effect of suppressing productivity; it is also fundamentally deflationary.

One could therefore argue that central banks should move away from inflation targeting and instead focus on misallocated capital – i.e. raise interest rates if capital misallocation is deemed too high.

You may ask the valid question – how high is too high?

In an economy where capital is allocated appropriately, property prices rise in line with the increase in labour productivity and debt-to-GDP doesn't increase[85], so that's my answer to you.

Targeting capital misallocation instead of inflation would almost certainly improve productivity; however, there is a twist. A rapidly ageing populace will, in the years to come, increase the capital required to service the elderly. From an economic point of view, that is also deemed a misallocation of capital, but it is still required. One would therefore have to distinguish between different sources of misallocation.

Fiscal policy

As I have alluded to several times already, increased infrastructure spending would have an immediate, and positive, impact on productivity, and hence on GDP growth, partly because the G in the GDP formula I introduced in chapter 3 would rise instantly, and partly because of the multiplier effect. As the infrastructure is improved, productivity will also improve in subsequent years.

Let me give you a simple example. If you travel to almost any major European country, you will see double-decker commuter trains with reasonable amounts of space, even at the busiest of times, but not in Britain.

Why is that?

The political leadership in the UK suffers from a narrow-minded attitude towards transportation (and the Brits are not alone in making this mistake). Labour productivity could be raised dramatically, if millions of commuters didn't waste all those hours in traffic jams every day. However, cars are a source of revenue for the government (due to petrol taxes), whereas trains are not. Hence vast amounts of money are spent every year on expanding the motorway system, while the railroad network is left outdated.

---

[85]   Source: The MacroStrategy Partnership LLP (2017,4).

Few would disagree that a better infrastructure enhances the productive potential of the economy, but there are two caveats[86]. Firstly, the political decision-making process often leads to bad decisions, which results in more infrastructure not always leading to a productivity-enhancing infrastructure.

Secondly, and partly as a result of the first issue, there is little robust evidence of a systematic link between the level of infrastructure spending and economic growth. It is therefore next to impossible to document any correlation between the two, which just goes to show that too much public money is spent on political pet projects (i.e. vote-winning projects) and not on projects that make economic sense.

Automation

In the eyes of many investors, an increased use of advanced robotics in the years to come is what is going to have the biggest positive impact on productivity. In chapter 9, I referred to BofAML's research paper from 2015 on advanced robotics[87], and I pointed out that the driver is first mover advantage.

Take the car manufacturing industry. At the time of BofAML's paper, an American spot welder was paid on average about $25 per hour. A robot could do the same job for $8 an hour (all in). Those countries that don't embrace the new technology will simply be left behind, such are the advantages, argue the researchers from BofAML (exhibit 10.2).

Developed economies have a massive advantage over China in this respect. China, because of the sheer number of people, cannot allow robots to replace hundreds of millions of workers. There are simply too many mouths to feed every day.

The old world has exactly the opposite problem. A shrinking workforce will force robots to be installed if we want to keep industry alive, partly because we won't have enough people to fill the manufacturing floors,

---

86 Source: IEA (2016).
87 BofAML (2015).

and partly because those who are left will be too expensive to do the job. The best line of defence against Chinese competition is therefore likely to be more automation.

Exhibit 10.2: Number of multi-purpose industrial robots (all types) per 10,000 employees in the manufacturing industry, 2015

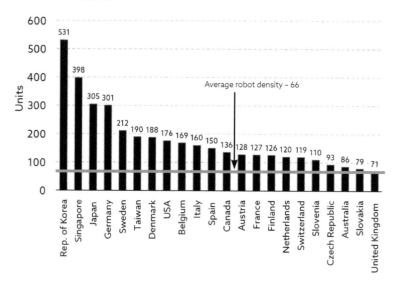

Source: International Federation of Robotics (2017).

A likely side effect of increased automation is low (possibly negative) inflation. Modest inflation is a desirable outcome, but deflation certainly isn't when we are about to drown in debt. The researchers from BofAML reckon that, whilst robots have on average become 27% cheaper over the last 10 years, they will fall a further 20%+ over the next ten years.

All this has the potential to boost productivity, and could be the saving grace for a number of otherwise doomed mature economies. How quickly it will all happen remains to be seen, but it is beyond doubt that automation will be a *massive* theme in the years to come.

Finally, two comments on the impact technology is having on productivity.

Firstly, although we can probably all agree that technology has changed the way many of us conduct our lives, it would be a grave mistake to assume that it has had a profound impact on productivity (hence on GDP growth). Assuming gross profits plus wages add up to a company's contribution to GDP (which is largely correct), one can measure how much Apple, Facebook and Netflix between them contributed to global GDP last year, and the answer is a woeful ¼%.[88]

Secondly, there is one major misconception amongst investors. Whereas many believe automation will only affect manufacturing, the reality is dramatically different. Take a simple example – education. A single professor can now, through digital technology, teach a course to millions of students simultaneously.

A new energy form

The ultimate solution to our productivity problems, though, is not automation but access to a new and cheaper energy form. Back in chapter 7, I introduced you to the concept of exergy, and why rising exploration and production costs are detrimental to productivity – not just in the energy sector but across the economy. Hence it goes without saying that a relatively simple solution to our productivity problem would be if we could gain access to a cheaper energy form.

Now, what is simple in principle, is not always that simple in practice. Scientists thought for many years that traditional nuclear power provided the answer to our energy problems, but various safety issues have never been satisfactorily addressed. Consequently, the technology has never been fully endorsed by the public.

That said, there is another nuclear energy form in the offing. Instead of separating nuclear particles, as you do in nuclear power plants today (a

---

[88]   Source: The MacroStrategy Partnership LLP (2017,5). See 'The problem in a nutshell (second take)' below for more on this topic.

technology called fission), you make nuclear particles collide, and that technology is called fusion.

What is fusion?

Fusion is the most basic form of energy in the universe. It is what powers the sun and the stars, where energy is produced by a nuclear reaction in which two atoms of the same lightweight element, usually an isotope of hydrogen, combine into a single molecule of helium[89].

When scientists attempt to replicate that process, the most important ingredients are sea water and lithium, both of which are in ample supply; hence vast amounts of energy could be produced at a very reasonable cost – at least theoretically. Even better, the fusion process does not suffer from all the safety issues that accompany traditional nuclear power. So far so good, but there is a problem – and a big one at that.

Researchers can produce plenty of energy from fusion but not in a controlled way. The best example is the hydrogen bomb, where a huge amount of energy is released in a highly destructive manner. If the same amount of energy could be released gradually – in a controlled manner – we would have found the eternal solution to planet Earth's energy requirements.

We would have virtually unlimited access to cheap energy, and greenhouse gasses would be a thing of the past. There would be little nuclear waste, and productivity would rise dramatically across the world, effectively dealing with the debt overhang. These factors in combination would resolve some of the biggest challenges mankind is faced with today.[90]

---

[89] Source RP Siegel (2012).

[90] The greenhouse gas problem could also be addressed by accelerating the implementation of renewable energy forms, but that wouldn't address our desperate need for cheaper energy, as renewables are still comparatively expensive.

Having said that, creating a controlled fusion reaction has proven very difficult. Because the nuclei have the same charge, they will electrically repel each other. To overcome the natural repulsion of the nuclei, you must give them sufficient energy. That means heating them up to about 12 million degrees but, as you heat a gas or plasma up, it expands and the atoms move further apart.

The trick is to contain the heated plasma long enough that the nuclei have the chance to collide and overcome the repulsive force. Researchers have now reached that point and have achieved energy breakeven, but there is still a long way to go, before the technology can be rolled out commercially.

The race against time

As you may recall from chapter 7, I made the point that the cost of producing fossil fuels continues to rise. As it becomes ever more expensive to deliver energy to the end-user, productivity growth will continue to slow, and GDP growth will ultimately turn negative.

Now, negative GDP growth would not be an insurmountable problem, if it weren't for two issues:

1. We won't be able to service the debt we are saddled with, so the ship will sink.

2. Longevity will almost certainly begin to fall.

The first issue is discussed in detail throughout this book, but the second one I haven't touched on before, so let me explain. The Industrial Revolution enabled the global population to expand dramatically. At the height of it, about 200 years ago, there were only 1 billion people in the world, and now there are 7.5 billion.

The productivity growth of the Industrial Revolution created capital of which human capital was part. If the economy begins to shrink, then the capital stock will also shrink, with human capital part of that. Declining longevity is a trend we had better get used to. Longevity has declined more recently in parts of the US and the UK, as we cannot afford the best – but also the most expensive – treatment forms. Access to very cheap energy could turn into an important lifeline in more than one sense.

If governments around the world were half as smart as they claim to be, research budgets into commercialising fusion would be multiplied. It is by far the best medication for a global economy in decay. Fusion will almost certainly have a much more dramatic effect on productivity and hence on GDP growth than anything automation can ever deliver.

However, it is a race against time. The global economy could quite possibly sink well before fusion reaches a state where commercialisation becomes viable, a point we won't reach for many years. Researchers say fusion on a commercial scale is still 30 years away, but researchers said the same 30 years ago. Hence the need for more research resources.

One final point to bear in mind. As fusion is rolled out on a grand scale, fossil fuel prices will fall dramatically. Coal prices will most likely go to $0, and so will natural gas prices, as coal and gas are both used almost exclusively for transportation and for heating our homes.

Oil is used somewhat differently than other fossil fuels. About 55% is used for transportation and about 20% for heating. That leaves about 25%, which is mostly used by the chemical industry (e.g. for plastics). The need for the 75% will vanish but not the remaining 25%. Consequently, I don't expect oil prices to go all the way to $0 – at least not in our lifetime – even if they are likely to weaken quite substantially.

Could inflation do the trick?

Strangely enough, a bout of inflation could also do a great deal to solve our productivity problem. The logic is straightforward. Excessive levels of debt ruin productivity. As debt climbs to unsustainable levels, there is only one way to dig ourselves out of the hole – *debt destruction*.

Debt destruction can happen in two ways – either through default or through high inflation. The former we experienced in the Great Depression in the 1930s and again in the Global Financial Crisis in

2007–09. The best example of the latter is probably the secular bear market of 1966–81.

If central banks were willing to deliberately stay behind the curve for a while, significant amounts of debt destruction would take place, just as it did in 1966–81. Phrased differently, for debt destruction to happen through inflation, you need central banks to play along, which they might just do.

Considering the environment we are in, and all the problems that come with that, such a strategy may not be as far-fetched as you may think. The Fed was never overly hawkish under Yellen's stewardship, and may turn out to be even more dovish under Jerome Powell. Adding to that, President Trump could also impact the overall balance at the Federal Reserve with the new appointments lined up during his presidency.

The Bank of England, with a very dovish ECB in its backyard, can't afford to be too hawkish, unless it is prepared to ruin the competitiveness of British industry.

Meanwhile, the ECB is not likely to change its dovish approach anytime soon. The southern part of the Eurozone is not out of the woods yet, and the ECB knows that setting rates at a level that would be suitable for the north could lead to other EU countries doing what the UK did in 2016.

The possibility of a more serious bout of inflation should therefore not be entirely dismissed.

The problem in a nutshell (second take)

Having said all of that, there is an altogether different way to approach the challenge of declining productivity and GDP growth. Not only is it different; it is also far more optimistic, as it puts events of recent years in a very different light. Martin Feldstein, professor of economics at Harvard University, is a proponent of this philosophy, and no book on the topic of declining GDP growth would be complete without at least a mention of Feldstein's ideas.

I should point out that Martin Feldstein is not just another attention-seeking wannabe. He is one of the very best economists ever to have planted his feet on this planet, so one should take his thoughts very seriously.

Martin Feldstein's story begins by asking a number of randomly selected people if they are better or worse off than they were years ago – before smartphones started to control our lives, before emails allowed us to deal with important issues in minutes rather than days or weeks, and before airbags became a standard feature in every car – a feature that has saved millions of lives. When asked the question that way, few people would argue that living standards have deteriorated in recent years.

Now, ask the same people the same question, but this time focus on the overall economy – is it better or worse off than, say, 20 years ago? The majority will now give you a very different answer – something along the lines of "I am not sure, but probably worse off", and some will even say that things have definitely deteriorated.

How come so many people feel their own life has improved91, yet they think the economy sucks?

Apart from the fact that GDP is a poor measure of living standards, the only logical explanation is that real GDP growth, the way it is currently calculated, is measured incorrectly, or so Martin Feldstein argues.

Going back to exhibit 5.1, we learned that GDP equals price times quantity when aggregated across all goods and services (jointly called products in this context). Q is easy to measure; it is the number of products sold over the period. P is also easy to measure, provided the product in question is the same from one period to the next. Problems arise if the quality of the product has changed, or if a new product has been introduced.

---

91   In this context, the painful subject of falling real wages (i.e. falling living standards – at least in nominal terms) in certain countries is being conveniently ignored.

How do you measure the value created by the improved/new product?

This is where hedonic regression comes in[92]. The statisticians in charge of the national accounts assess the value of the new, improved product and make the necessary adjustments. For example, when colour TVs were first introduced, they were priced significantly more expensively than black & white TVs, but the quality was deemed so much better that the full price increase never found its way into inflation statistics.

So far so good, but there is a problem, Feldstein says. Unless the cost of making the new, improved product has gone up, the quality of the product cannot possibly have improved, or so argues the US Bureau of Labor Statistics[93], which oversees measuring and reporting US inflation. This effectively means that, in these digital times where many products are improved at no added cost, and sometimes even at a reduced cost, many product improvements are unaccounted for in the national accounts.

It is widely recognised that products like Google offer value to the user without being properly recognised in the national accounts, so the problem is known; however, few people realise that the problem goes way beyond companies like Google. As Feldstein points out, if our statisticians only recognise quality improvements, if the price on the product has been raised, the problem is much bigger than most people realise.

Feldstein's key argument is that the existing methodology – which is used across the world – measures the cost of production – i.e. the input factors – much better than it does the value to the consumer – i.e. the final output – and that affects the national accounts *big time*.

Feldstein further argues that inflation is *much* lower than the numbers published by the US Bureau of Labor Statistics would suggest, and that real GDP growth since the 1970s should probably be increased by

---

92   Hedonic regression is a method of valuing a product by breaking it into its constituent parts and then estimating the contribution of each part.

93   Although Feldstein's comments are US specific, most other countries use the same approach when calculating inflation.

about 2% *per annum*, if one were to make appropriate adjustments for quality improvements. That would certainly explain why consumers are so much more upbeat about their own living standards than they are about the overall economy.

It would also at least partly explain why everything has slowed to a trickle; it would certainly explain why GDP growth is so low, and why productivity has hardly changed in recent years.

The solution?

A more appropriate way to adjust for quality improvement or, as Feldstein would say, a different approach to hedonic regression.

One could even conclude (as Feldstein does) that the current methodology translates into unnecessary pessimism, anti-globalisation, and even a widespread distrust of government that leads to extreme views (think Marine Le Pen in France). Consequently, one shouldn't just consider it an academic exercise that we ought to get right for the sake of printing a more precise picture of the national accounts. The ramifications are much more serious than that.

Critique of Feldstein's approach

Feldstein's critique of hedonic pricing, as it is practised today, is both right and wrong. On one hand, I would agree that it is nonsense not to consider quality improvements, unless the cost of making the new, improved product has gone up.

On the other hand, there is a significant risk of double counting when applying hedonic principles. Let me explain (and this is just one of many examples).

Think of somebody who is dependent on his laptop when doing his work, say a research analyst. A more powerful laptop would likely lead to an increase in output from the analyst in question, but that is already included in his contribution to GDP. If you also assign the value of the increased output to the computer firm because the laptop is faster now, you count the improvement twice, which is obviously not correct.

Consequently, by following Feldstein's ideas, you could end up overestimating GDP rather than underestimating it. Having said that, I think most would agree that, in these digital times, GDP is a terrible measure of living standards whatever way it is calculated.

11
What's Next?

I have a hunch that my vision of improved productivity, which I have just shared with you, is nothing more than wishful thinking, at least for a number of years. That said, things are rarely black or white; the true colour is almost always some shade of grey, hence my reluctance to turn outright apocalyptic at this stage, although there are indeed some very good reasons why the future looks bleak. This chapter provides my take on what is likely to happen next, assuming no miracle cure is round the corner.

The high cost of servicing the elderly

U P TO THIS point, the picture I have painted is not particularly encouraging, although there are bright spots in between, which have the potential to lift the sombre tone. I am thinking of the feedback loop from a stronger East, the potentially positive impact from increased automation, and the possibility that fusion energy finally arrives and dramatically reduces our dependence on fossil fuels.

That said, the clouds gathering in the horizon are indeed rather dark. As far as demographics are concerned, in this book, I have focused mostly on the negative effects on GDP growth from a shrinking workforce, and have only briefly referred to the rising cost of servicing the elderly. In the years to come, that could possibly become the biggest issue of them all. Think back to chapter 10 and the possibility of declining longevity. That will not go down very well amongst us baby boomers, who are used to uninterrupted progress.

Let me share with you a statistic which has caused me a few sleepless nights. According to the United Nations, life expectancy in developed economies will rise from 78.3 in 2015 to 81.4 by 2035 – largely due to reduced smoking and better healthcare – which is all good. However, the IMF reckons that a 3-year extension to life expectancies would increase debt-to-GDP by 50%, as it is incredibly expensive to keep us alive those few years longer.

Can we afford for debt-to-GDP to rise another 50% from already elevated levels? No, and the only conclusions I can reach are the following:

1. Unless governments take drastic action, the ship *will* sink. It is only a question of time.

2. One such drastic action could be for authorities to either withhold information about new medical treatment forms (as they already do on a limited scale in the UK[94]), or simply refuse to pay for new and better treatments.

3. If you want to live longer than your parents, you will need to be either wealthy or well informed about new treatment forms – and probably both.

The rising cost of healthcare, and the rising cost of energy exploration and production, are two of the biggest challenges facing mankind today, at least from a financial point of view. As per current entitlements, the cost in the US of providing Social Security, Medicare and Medicaid will grow by almost $100bn from 2017 to 2018 alone and will, because of ageing, grow by a mindboggling $2 trillion[95] (over 10% of 2017 US GDP) over the next 10 years.

---

94 The National Health Service in the UK does not always inform you about the more expensive treatment forms. I have experienced this myself.
95 Source: Daniel Amerman (2017).

A couple of critical questions

I just referred to the country with the best demographic profile of them all – the US. Let's turn to a region with one of the worst – Europe. With a shrinking European workforce in mind, short of any automation miracle, or short of the scientists finally figuring out how to deliver fusion energy in a controlled manner, I find it hard to see where any meaningful European GDP growth is going to come from[96]. That raises (at least) two questions:

1. Does GDP growth matter at the end of the day?

2. How much debt can we afford before the entire ship sinks?

The answer to the first question depends on where you live, and what your current living standards are, I suppose. I have discussed this topic with friends and family in Denmark, and the prevailing view appears to be that living standards are now so good that we don't need to aim for more. We just need to protect what we already have.

More spare time; more time with the family; time to go and watch little Johnny play his first football match rather than working those extra few hours – where the tax man keeps most of it anyway – is increasingly becoming the attitude amongst the people I speak to.

That said, it would be terribly narrow-minded to assume that everyone is happy with things the way they are. Even in relatively affluent countries around the world, millions of people strive for a better life, and to all those people GDP growth matters.

I should also add that, in one critical respect, robust GDP growth matters a great deal. With debt-to-GDP across mature economies approaching 400%, debt is fast becoming a ticking time bomb, and there is only one way to avoid the ship from sinking. GDP *must* continue to grow at a robust rate. Otherwise we simply cannot service that much debt.

---

96   As I have pointed out earlier in the book, the workforce will shrink in many, but not in all, European countries.

In that context, let's re-visit one of President Trump's election promises. If he is going to deliver on his promise to the US electorate to grow the US economy by at least 3.5% annually under his stewardship, assuming a constant 20% 'return' on added debt[97], he must add at least $3.3 trillion of new debt *every year* to an already highly leveraged US balance sheet. Sounds to me like a non-starter. 3.5% annual GDP growth in the US on a sustained basis is simply not going to happen.

Moreover, the only way Trump can be certain the economy will continue to grow *at all* in the years to come is by letting in more immigrants, and the same could be said about most other developed countries. The US workforce will decline significantly over the next 20 years, if you include only those born in the US with US parents (exhibit 11.1). This would obviously be a rather dramatic U-turn on his declared policy on immigration, but low or no immigration would most likely be massively damaging to economic growth.

Exhibit 11.1: Change in US working age population (those aged 25–64) in %

	1965–74	1975–84	1985–94	1995–04	2005–14	2015–24	2025–35
Immigrants	1.0	3.8	6.9	10.8	6.1	3.5	1.2
U.S. born with immigrant parents	−2.5	−3.1	−1.8	0.3	2.4	5.7	7.9
U.S. born with U.S. born parents	13.3	20.0	15.1	10.6	4.8	−4.3	−3.8

Source: Pew Research Center (2017).

---

97   As I have mentioned earlier, in recent years, US GDP has only grown by about $0.20 for every dollar of additional debt.

Pew Research Center's projections suggest that 17.6 million new immigrants will be added to the US working-age population by 2035. Without them, the number of working-age immigrants would decline by 2035, and the total US working-age population would drop by almost 8 million (or more than 4%) from 2015 levels.

Have we reached an inflection point?

Going back to the gist of this book – a mix of structural trends driving everything lower – is it possible that at least some of those trends have reached an inflection point? Take demographics. As I showed in chapter 4 (exhibit 4.4.3), as people reach a certain age, bonds don't do so well anymore, and the reason is simple.

Savings peak when people are middle-aged. At that age, most people – at least those in Anglo-Saxon countries – favour equities over bonds. As they age further, they increasingly switch from equities to bonds in preparation for retirement. Once retired, they live on their savings, hence they become net sellers of both bonds and equities. What has been a very conducive environment for bonds for several years could turn on its head (if it hasn't already done so), and the headwinds could gradually become more and more severe.

I bring this up in the context of the various structural trends being discussed in this book, as it is indeed possible that interest rates will begin to creep upwards despite the overall economy not doing particularly well.

Likewise, migration could also have hit an inflection point. One of the less admirable aspects of human behaviour these days is the growing sense of nationalism. There is absolute nothing wrong about being proud of your origin – and I am certainly proud of being Danish – but I have a big problem when I can smell 1930s-style nationalism on the march again, and I can.

If the massive influx of Eastern Europeans into Western Europe has hit an inflection point – and early signs would suggest it may have – there are several implications. GDP growth will slow even further (if possible), but workers' bargaining power will improve, which could lead to a shift back from capital to labour, in terms of how national income is divided between the two. Such a shift would obviously be bad for corporate profitability as well as equity returns, and inflation would also begin to rise again, should it happen.

The combined outlook of only modest nominal GDP growth and rising inflation – and therefore also rising interest rates – is not the best cocktail for a heavily indebted European continent. And the Brits, whilst busy celebrating the "non-event" of Brexit (or so they think), will soon come to realise that just because they have left the EU, they haven't at all escaped the structural issues discussed in this book.

The era of neo-nationalism

Talking about growing nationalism, let me quickly sum up how the global economy has developed over the past half century. As I have already mentioned, following World War II, the developed world underwent a transportation revolution, and we converted from coal to electricity. Consequently, the economy grew exceptionally fast over a 10-year period from the mid-1950s to the mid-1960s (exhibit 1.1).

Towards the end of that era, the Cuban crisis erupted, and the world suddenly found itself engulfed in what became known as the Cold War. Later that decade the Vietnam War would take its toll, and two oil crises in the 1970s would ensure that the entire period from 1966 to 1981 would go down in history as one of the most difficult for financial markets.

As we moved further into the 1980s, the sentiment changed. Reagan and Thatcher had assumed power in the US and UK respectively, and large parts of the public sector were privatised. The change in mood was noticeable and, consequently, we entered 35 years of optimism – a period I would call the era of neo-liberalism.

The Global Financial Crisis changed all that. People became more inward looking as many felt insecure with real wages and living standards under pressure in many countries. The era of neo-nationalism was born.

Neo-nationalism is driven by the stagnating (or even declining) spending power of the majority of the workforce. As a foreigner in the UK (as I am), I suddenly feel I have to justify my presence when speaking to strangers. ("Where do you come from? Why are you here?") Never before have I encountered that attitude.

Neo-nationalism will (at best) lead to more economic growth infringements, such as rising trade tariffs between nations. Lower GDP growth will in turn lead to lower growth in corporate profitability, and a rising share of national income going to labour at the expense of capital.

Remember the point I made in chapter 8? That wealth-to-GDP (capital-to-output) will likely mean revert in the years to come? As I pointed out, since the beginning of the neo-liberal era, capital has taken an ever-rising share of national income. Could the era of neo-nationalism be the catalyst that sets the mean reverting train in motion? I think so.

The end of monetary policy?

Ever since the back of inflation was broken with a spell of extraordinarily high interest rates in the late 1970s and early 1980s, inflation targeting has been at the centre of monetary policy, and 2% annual inflation has been deemed the desirable level – at least in more mature economies. With several structural trends continuing to drive inflation down, one could argue (and I do) that inflation targeting should be shelved – at least temporarily.

The inflation targeting approach has had the effect of large amounts of capital being misallocated every year – capital that could, and should, have been used productively, has instead been used unproductively. The best example of that would probably be property speculation, such as the buy-to-let boom in the UK, or building bridges to nowhere in China.

The only conclusion I can reach is that, in a low-inflation environment caused by structural factors, a monetary policy programme centered around inflation targeting is bound to misfire. The focus should instead be on misallocated capital, and interest rates should be raised when too much capital is misallocated.

How does one measure how much capital is misallocated?

Admittedly, there is no simple way to do it, but there is a roundabout way, which I alluded to in chapter 10. Think of how much debt you need to add to grow GDP by $1. Years ago, it was normal for GDP and debt to grow dollar for dollar, but that has all changed. Nowadays, the most indebted countries grow GDP by no more than 20 cents for every dollar of debt they add. Central bankers could (and should) draw a line in the sand somewhere.

You may recall my mention of Jan Tinbergen in chapter 9. Which university today's political leaders and central bankers attended I don't know, but they were certainly fast asleep when Tinbergen's findings were discussed. Somehow they all started to believe that monetary policy can sort out every problem from A to Z, which it clearly cannot.

Back to my point about inflection points. I believe we have reached the end of the road as far as monetary policy is concerned. I am not suggesting that central bankers won't move policy rates up and down anymore, as they see fit – of course they will – but monetary policy will increasingly be supplemented by other policy tools – first and foremost fiscal policy.

Recent government noise would suggest that this is already on the radar screen in both the US and UK, and it will be interesting to see how it all pans out in the years to come. My guess is that policy rates will be changed more frequently – and more symmetrically.

That is not at all bad for economic stability, as long as our American friends stop buying into the belief that the Fed's *raison d'être* is to bail out financial investors at any cost.

A few more words on debt destruction

I first presented the concept of debt destruction in chapter 10. Debt destruction is the inevitable outcome of debt super-cycles. Well, at least so far, it has always been. Debt destruction happens when the ship is so overloaded that it starts to sink and, as I outlined in chapter 10, it can happen in two distinctly different ways.

Either the ship sinks with everybody still on board as it did in the 1930s and again in 2007–09, or debt is destroyed over a longer period of time through high inflation, as it happened in the secular bear market from 1966 to 1981. There has never been a benign end to debt super-cycles. *Never!*

However, there is always a first. I am sure many central bankers around the world are now praying for a world first. The consensus view amongst the investors I speak to is that the ship won't sink, as rising automation will improve productivity dramatically and ultimately save us all, and that is certainly possible.

What works against that is the fact that productivity rarely grows by more than 2% annually. It did so from the mid-1950s to the mid-1960s, but not even the technology revolution (digitalisation, internet, etc.) around the millennium resulted in more than 2% annual productivity growth. No other period comes even close.

Given the poor projections for workforce growth in the years to come, would that be enough to prevent the ship from sinking – at least in some countries? I don't think so. I therefore conclude that if automation is the best game changer we can come up with, there is further trouble lined up – not necessarily tomorrow, but eventually. We have learned from Japan that central bankers have lots of tricks up their sleeves, and that the show can go on for much longer than any of us ever thought possible.

That leaves one option only, assuming we all beg for a benign outcome, and that is fusion energy. Now, that would be a game changer, and almost certainly the biggest game changer ever. Having access to virtually unlimited amounts of energy at a very reasonable cost would change *everything*, just like the structural trends discussed in this book are likely to change everything.

When I say *energy at a very reasonable cost*, I need to explain. Once a commercial fusion plant is up and running, the cost of producing an extra GWh of electricity will almost certainly be next to nothing. However, the cost of establishing those plants could quite possibly be prohibitively high; another reason why we need to steady the ship now. It would be sad if we couldn't afford the conversion to fusion, once it finally arrives.

Delay and Pray

At this point I should point out that there is indeed another possible outcome – an outcome I would describe as *extend and pretend* or perhaps *delay and pray*, which broadly speaking is the economic policy being pursued at present.

Central bankers all over the world – with one eye on Japan – hope they can muddle through, and they could possibly be right. Automation could quite conceivably stimulate economic growth enough that muddling through becomes a viable outcome – at least until fusion energy walks through the door and saves our bacon.

Why one eye on Japan? Japan has taught central bankers a very important lesson in recent years; that extend and pretend can work wonders for a long time, provided you sell your story convincingly enough. The demographic outlook in Japan is nothing short of horrific. As of the latest count, there are 126 million people in Japan. By 2050, there will be 107 million left, and by 2100 they will be down to 83 million[98].

A decline of that magnitude is destined to have an immense impact on everyday life in Japan, but that is not my point. The point is, as you saw in exhibit 4.10, several European countries are not that far behind

---

98   Source: United Nations (2015).

Japan in terms of the number of the most expensive elderly – those aged 80 and over.

Of the major European countries, the ones in the best shape demographically are France and the UK and, globally, the US is in pole position. I am sure those three countries will all muddle through. Having said that, others won't be able to. For a country like Italy, the combination of *desperately* poor demographics, low productivity, and an unhealthy amount of indebtedness, almost certainly spells trouble down the road. How the political leadership choose to deal with that will to a large degree determine how financial markets react.

How to stimulate demand

I still refuse to jump on the bandwagon and predict the end of the world as we know it. Over the years, I have learned that things are rarely either black or white. As a matter of fact, if we weren't so indebted, I wouldn't worry too much about the bleak demographic outlook. As the Swiss have learned, you don't need much GDP growth to prosper. That said, the Swiss haven't done what many Anglo-Saxons have – loaded up on debt, enjoyed a lifestyle they couldn't afford, only to hope it would all work itself out in the end.

However, the combination of ageing, excessive debt levels and stagnant real wage growth has got trouble painted all over it. Economic growth theory would suggest that, unless we can make aggregate demand grow faster than aggregate supply, GDP growth will ultimately turn negative, and the reason is relatively straightforward.

As you may recall from exhibit 5.1, the starting point for calculating GDP is price times quantity (P x Q) of goods and services changing hands across the economy. The combination of ageing, high debts and falling real wages have led to the D-curve shifting out more slowly than the S-curve and, when that happens, prices come under pressure, and GDP growth slows down. Exhibit 11.2 illustrates why that is. As you can see, the impact on pricing is only disinflationary to begin with but, ultimately, deflation kicks in – which has already started to happen in some countries.

Exhibit 11.2: Inflation outlook when supply grows faster than demand

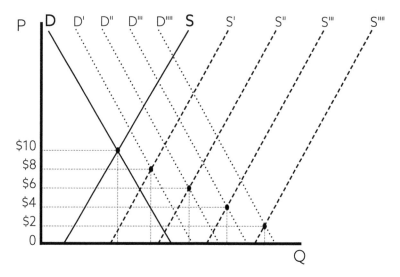

Source: Strategic Economic Decisions (2016).

Governments need to understand this dynamic; why it is important for the D-curve to shift out faster than the S-curve. Narrow-minded political leaders blame globalisation for the S-curve having shifted out so sharply in recent years, and the man in the street agrees.

Whilst correct that globalisation has indeed had some impact, the argument fails on two accounts. Firstly, it entirely ignores the positive impact growing international trade has had on economic growth and, secondly, it disregards the impact more advanced technology has had on the S-curve.

In my opinion, the S-curve has shifted out so dramatically primarily because of that, and those in charge of setting the political agenda should focus on what is easiest to affect. That would imply policies designed to push the D-curve out faster rather than trying to hold the

S-curve back – something they cannot do much about anyway, unless they want to hold technology improvements back.

Could Martin Feldstein be on to something?

On the other hand, could Martin Feldstein be on to something? If his estimates are anywhere near correct, what's the problem? Why don't we just change the way we do the national accounts and live happily ever thereafter?

I would certainly agree with him that only accounting for quality improvements if the price has been increased is wrong. In these digital times, many goods and services are improved regularly without the price being touched at all. On the other hand, double counting is no good.

That said, whether GDP growth is underestimated or overestimated doesn't change the fact that it will be punitively expensive to service the growing number of elderly in the years to come.

Moreover, Feldstein's ideas don't change the fact that debt levels are unsustainably high, and that vast amounts of capital that could – and should – be used productively is instead used to service existing debt. On the other hand, it could explain why we continue to get away with having so much debt. The economy is quite simply doing better than we all think it is, or at least that is what Feldstein argues.

I would agree with Feldstein that a new approach is warranted, even if I (intuitively) think that the 2% he suggests annual GDP growth is underestimated by is on the high side. Having said that, debt levels are now so high that accidents will almost certainly happen, should interest rates rise even modestly.

Hence I think the ship *will* sink in some countries, but that it is likely to stay afloat in others. To avoid any mayhem across the OECD, the pension model must change, though. My guesstimate – and it is only that – is that the DB model will disappear altogether; a transfer from DB to DC will become mandatory. It is simply too expensive to keep

DB alive. However, it won't happen until the ship is about to sink, as it is clearly not a vote winner.

A spoiled generation

Eliminating something people have come to believe is a human right – such as DB pension schemes – will undoubtedly cause problems. The problem in a nutshell is that we are dealing with the most spoiled generation *ever;* a generation born in the first 20 years following World War II; a generation that has enjoyed unparalleled success and only ever experienced good times.

Before I upset too many readers, I should probably point out that it is also my generation and, more importantly, it is the generation in power today. Most heads of companies, and most senior government officials, belong to this generation.

When I look around, I spot plenty of people who are used to getting everything they want. Many of these people simply don't understand the meaning of the word *no*, and because they have been spoiled rotten for many years, many haven't looked after themselves properly. Many – at least in the UK where I live – don't even have any retirement savings to speak of. "Nothing to worry about", they say. "That will be taken care of." And that is the generation running the world today!

The root cause

I started the book by saying that when the debt super-cycle reaches the end of the road, when baby boomers retire in large numbers, and when the middle classes in the developed world suddenly suffer from declining living standards, there is most definitely a root cause.

So, what is that root cause?

I hope I have made it clear by now that it is not a single factor but a combination of factors that have led to the current malaise. Ageing has unquestionably played a role, but ageing will almost certainly play an even bigger role over the next few decades – particularly in South Korea,

Japan and continental Europe, where the outlook is most troubling. Likewise, rising debt levels have also impacted productivity growth negatively and thus held back economic growth.

Adding to that, stagnating – or even declining – living standards in the developed world have further reduced demand for goods and services. In other words, if there is a root cause, it is the fact that the D-curve for years has shifted out more slowly than the S-curve. See chapter 5 again for an in-depth discussion of this issue.

Bring in the helicopters

Reversing that trend is relatively simple. *All* you need to do is to stimulate demand in the developed world. Let me wrap up this chapter by providing one or two simple examples as to how that could be achieved.

Start by bringing in the helicopters. In the UK, many (mostly young and almost always poorly educated) people think government's sole role in life is to ensure they can enjoy a comfortable life without ever having to work. I don't know what these people are called in other countries, but in Britain we call them career benefit seekers.

Reduce entitlements dramatically, but introduce negative tax rates on the lowest earned incomes to encourage these people to (re)join the workforce. Technically speaking, it is helicopter money, but it is helicopter money through fiscal means, and it will most definitely push the D-curve out without turning the country into another Zimbabwe.

Further up the food chain, you simply introduce an annual tax rebate for 2–3 years and monitor how that affects consumer spending. If it works, you let it run for as long as necessary, and you finance it by taxing multi-national companies' untaxed profits in offshore tax havens.

12

Why Index Investing Will Dwindle

Over the years, I have come across so many investors who claim to be long-term investors, only for them to have a panic attack the first time there is a bump in the road. I can promise you there are many bumps in the road in front of us, and I can also assure you that if my recommendations work well in the near term, it will be down to luck more than anything else.

The four different types of risk[99]

B EFORE I SHARE with you how I would structure my portfolio, given the not very encouraging conditions I have just laid out, I should offer a brief explanation as to what I think of the different types of risk one assumes when investing, and why that is of the utmost relevance as far as portfolio construction is concerned.

---

[99] James Montier of GMO provides a brilliant definition of risk which deserves to be mentioned: "Risk is the permanent loss of capital, never a number. In essence, and regrettably, the obsession with the quantification of risk (beta, standard deviation, VaR) has replaced a more fundamental, intuitive, and important approach to the subject. Risk clearly isn't a number. It is a multifaceted concept, and it is foolhardy to try to reduce it to a single figure."

First and foremost, I differentiate between behavioural patterns and drivers of risk. Behavioural patterns may drive shorter-term tactical decisions (e.g. whether to hedge the currency exposures or not), but they *never* drive my core portfolio construction. Furthermore, asset classes and types of investment vehicle are largely irrelevant and merely represent execution tools to get exposure to the different types of risks on offer.

I distinguish between four types of risk – beta, alpha, credit and gamma risk, all of which will be reviewed in the following. Before I do so, though, let me make one thing perfectly clear. What I am about to say is not at all the holy grail. There are many ways one can choose to approach portfolio construction. My way has worked well for me over the years, but it is not a choice between my way or the highway. There are indeed other ways you can do it.

Beta risk

Beta risk is market risk – plain and simple. I distinguish between equity beta, credit beta, etc., and it goes without saying that for beta risk to be quantifiable, the underlying asset(s) must be listed.

Returns from taking beta risk are primarily a function of how you choose to allocate your capital across different asset classes and countries, but the cost factor is also significant – particularly in a low return environment. As most active investors underperform passive investors once costs are taken into consideration, the most cost efficient way of getting exposure to beta risk is through passive investment vehicles such as ETFs.

All the structural trends that I have identified will significantly affect your beta return. For example, take demographics. We know that older consumers spend less than their younger peers do; hence ageing affects corporate profitability and therefore also equity returns.

You may recall a point I made earlier – that the low interest rates most of us have enjoyed in recent years, have led to considerable amounts of misallocated capital – capital that has been deployed unproductively. As far as beta risk is concerned, in the years to come, the key to superior beta returns will likely be to avoid those countries and sectors where the misallocation has been most pronounced. Obvious examples of that would include China and property worldwide.

One final point on beta risk. As I pointed out in chapter 2, equities perform vastly differently, depending on where we are in the monetary policy cycle. As we have entered a hiking cycle with Fed's decision to raise rates in December 2015, irrespective of the structural trends discussed in this book, there are very good reasons to believe that beta returns will be quite modest in the years to come.

Alpha risk

Alpha risk is non-market risk or, as it is often called, idiosyncratic risk, and alpha is a zero-sum game before costs. For every underperforming investor, there is always somebody who outperforms. When people say that nobody outperforms anymore, it is sheer nonsense. If somebody underperforms, somebody else *must* outperform (before costs).

Alpha returns are driven by extracting risk premia from mis-pricings in the listed markets, and there is no correlation to beta. Pure alpha is incredibly difficult to find in today's highly efficient markets, and only a fraction of the supposedly best investment managers – hedge fund managers – generates any (positive) alpha at all[100].

In the early days of the alternative investment industry – back in the 1980s and 1990s – it was possible to pick up a considerable amount of alpha by merely buying and selling the same security on different exchanges. If you think that sounds more like trading than investing, you are absolutely correct, but that is indeed how many hedge fund managers delivered superior returns back then.

---

[100] Last time I looked, only about 15% of the 11,000+ hedge funds generated any alpha.

That has all changed. The amount of alpha generated by hedge funds in recent years has been disappointingly low, and I think there are at least a couple of reasons for that.

Before I share those reasons with you, allow me to make a comment that might result in a few hostile reactions. If anything, hedge fund managers' performance stats more recently have proven they are not as smart as some people think they are (including themselves). They simply took advantage of inefficiencies whenever possible. Now, with most of those inefficiencies no longer there, it is obvious that they are mere mortals.

Anyway, back to my two reasons. Firstly, there is far more capital chasing mis-pricings today, making margins harder to come by and secondly, technology has changed dramatically. Algo-based trading now accounts for a large percentage of total volume on all major exchanges, and inefficiencies are harvested in nanoseconds rather than days or weeks, as we saw back in the golden years. However, alpha will not entirely disappear, as long as markets don't go up and down in straight lines.

Credit risk

Credit risk is precisely what it says on the tin. The risk is mostly, but not entirely, idiosyncratic, as the probability of default is largely a function of the borrower's financial conditions.

However, I don't always categorise credit risk as credit risk. Let me explain. If the government of a country suddenly introduces exchange controls, a domestic borrower with obligations to a non-domestic creditor may not be able to honour those obligations, even if his financial situation allows him to do so. I think of that as political risk and categorise it as gamma risk.

Gamma risk

Gamma risk is often associated with unlisted, less liquid investment strategies, which usually have a more convex return profile. Of all the gamma risks, the illiquidity premium is probably the one that has had the biggest impact on returns in recent years. Tie up your capital for several years, and suddenly (expected) returns are *much* higher, but there are obviously risks associated with such a strategy.

I often come across investment managers, who proudly tell me they generate plenty of alpha, but what those managers typically do has nothing whatsoever to do with alpha. They generate solid returns because they have identified a way to benefit from taking other risks such as illiquidity risk. From my experience, those managers who cannot articulate *precisely* which types of risk they are exposed to, and why they generate the returns they do, usually relinquish their excess returns sooner or later.

Gamma risk can also be employed in the liquid space, and the beauty of gamma risk is that you can turn that risk up or down as you see fit without it affecting your beta exposure. If you are active in listed equity markets, you have probably heard of investment strategies such as smart beta investing or factor-based investing. Think of the factors in factor-based investing as gamma risks.

Five of the most widely recognised factors in factor-based investing are volatility, momentum, income, value and size, but researchers have, over the years, identified more than 300 different factors[101], so you have plenty to choose from. The returns from the different factors vary significantly from year to year, i.e. the overall portfolio return may be greatly enhanced, if you can identify the factors in vogue (exhibit 12.1).

---

101   Source: Elroy Dimson, Paul Marsh and Mike Staunton (2017,1).

Exhibit 12.1: Post-crisis equity factor return premia (UK)

2008	2009	2010	2011	2012	2013	2014	2015	2016	2008–2016
Low vol 127.0	Size 24.9	Size 12.4	Low vol 35.0	Size 17.0	Mom 32.4	Mom 42.8	Low vol 23.7	Value 2 0.2	Mom 12.8
Mom 78.8	Income 1.1	Value 3.2	Income 28.3	Value 14.8	Size 15.5	Size 12.1	Mom 20.1	Income 15.3	Size 6.5
Income 15.7	Value -6.9	Mom 0.7	Mom 20.6	Mom -1.7	Low vol 11.5	Income -1.3	Size 11.1	Size -4.9	Low vol 5.5
Value -11.8	Low vol -20.1	Income -13.7	Size -4.9	Income -8.1	Income 0.0	Low vol -6.2	Income -11.2	Mom -18.3	Income 2.1
Size -17.5	Mom -25.4	Low vol -22.9	Value -10.7	Low vol -15.7	Value 0.0	Value -10.0	Value -20.9	Low vol -21.2	Value -3.2

Source: Elroy Dimson, Paul Marsh and Mike Staunton (2017,1). Copyright © 2017 Elroy Dimson, Paul Marsh and Mike Staunton. All rights reserved. Mom = momentum.

Where not to go

With those formalities sorted out, let's jump straight in at the deep end. I would keep my exposure to beta risk – whether credit beta or equity beta – quite low, at least until the world returns to some sort of normality (whatever that means), and that could take many years. Alpha returns are notoriously difficult to come by, so alpha risk is also low on my list of priorities. Credit risk and gamma risk are my top picks with the latter being my undisputed favourite at the moment.

How is it possible to like credit risk but not credit beta risk?

Credit beta is a risk factor you are mostly exposed to when investing in listed credit instruments. You can expose yourself to idiosyncratic credit risk in the private credit market without being (significantly) exposed to credit beta. There are many interesting investment opportunities on offer in the private credit space – royalties, leasing and regulatory capital relief[102] to mention a few.

---

[102] Where banks offload part of their loan book to long-term investors.

I am often confronted with the view that investors – particularly institutional investors – must invest *somewhere*, so what is there to worry about? With a largely dysfunctional government bond market, and a growing apathy towards hedge funds, equities are one of the only games in town for many investors, so why not take advantage of that?

Whilst somewhat sympathetic to that view, it ignores a simple but critically important fact. Even if most investors have never experienced anything like it (because they are not old enough), equities have a history of occasionally generating *very* negative real returns (exhibit 12.2) – and sometimes for long periods of time. If exhibit 12.2 doesn't convince you, I suggest you take another look at exhibit 2.2.

Exhibit 12.2: Periods with lowest equity returns

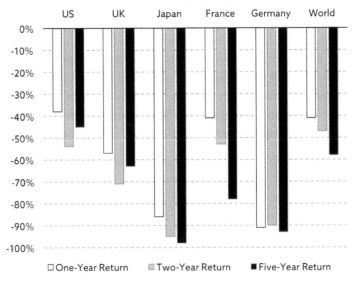

One cannot assume that the Fed (or any other central bank for that matter) will always be there to bail investors out, should another 2008 happen. Moreover, given the cascade of negative structural trends we will be faced with in the years to come, combined with the fact that we are now in a hiking cycle in the US and about to enter one in Europe, I would assign a relatively high probability to equity beta returns being negative in some countries for an extended period of time.

What sorts of beta returns can be expected?

Do I really expect equity beta returns to be negative for years to come? In a limited number of countries, yes, but certainly not everywhere. As you saw in chapter 2, real returns on global equities since 1900 have been around 5% annually whereas, during the Great Bull Market, average annual equity returns have been more than twice that.

The Great Bull Market benefitted immensely from the baby boomers moving into their peak spending years – a trend which is now in full reverse. I am therefore extremely confident in my prediction that the sorts of equity returns obtained during the last century (1900–2016) will prove the top end of the range of returns which can be expected in the years to come. Few countries will do better than that over the next 20–30 years, and some will do (significantly) worse. On average, I would expect beta exposure to deliver 0–3% real returns annually.

My favourite country to struggle is Italy. The combination of a rapidly ageing populace, poor public finances, falling real wages[103] and a culture of anti-authoritarianism has got problems spelled all over it. In the past, Italy devalued regularly to maintain a reasonable level of competitiveness but, being in the Eurozone, such a strategy is no longer an option. Exactly when all the wheels come off is hard to say but, when it happens, recent problems in Greece will look like a walk in the park.

Germany, on the other hand, is in a much better place, despite the two countries sharing largely the same demographic profile. Angela Merkel's decision to allow many migrants to settle in her country, combined with a rapidly rising penetration of industrial robots (see exhibit 10.2 again)

---

[103] Only one European country has experienced a bigger decline in real wages (i.e. in living standards) this millennium, and that is the UK.

and very strong public finances could quite possibly make the ageing of the German populace manageable.

Moreover, Germany's commitment to industrial robots will further enhance German industry's already sublime level of competitiveness, making the German equity market one of my favourite candidates to outperform global averages in the years to come.

I expect nothing extraordinary from US equity markets – at least for the next 10 years or so, when US demographics begin to improve again (much sooner than European demographics will). My main concern as far as US equities are concerned is valuation. US equities are just *so* expensive. Having said that, as I have already pointed out, overvaluation can prevail for a long time, and it would be outright foolish of me to try and project when I think it will correct itself.

The UK market is in an extraordinary situation because of Brexit, which may push some of the fundamental issues discussed in this book to the back burner – at least temporarily. One thing is certain, though. Issues to do with Brexit will be with us for many years to come. Those who believe everything will settle down once we have left the EU are in for a rather rude awakening. Article 50 was invoked on the 29th March, 2017, meaning that the UK will no longer be a member of the EU from the 29th March, 2019. Issues to do with that will stay with us for many years to come.

How UK equities will perform in that sort of environment is incredibly difficult to say. I hope the Brexiters are proven right when they say that a life outside the EU opens plenty of new doors, but I fear not. Despite running a persistent trade deficit with the rest of the EU, British industry is far more dependent on the EU (as a percentage of total exports) than the rest of the EU is on Britain. No free trade agreement between the two will turn me very negative on UK equities.

The gamma risk factors I fancy the most

The gamma risks I would prefer to be exposed to over the next 10 years are (from least to most favoured):

1. Size risk

2. Style risk

3. Income risk

4. Illiquidity risk

The style factor is best pursued in the liquid space. You can get exposure to size risk and income risk in both liquid and illiquid investment strategies, whereas you must always – surprise, surprise – go to the illiquid space to pick up the illiquidity premium.

Exhibit 12.3.1: Number of funds and AuM by size (in USD million) measured as % of hedge fund industry total

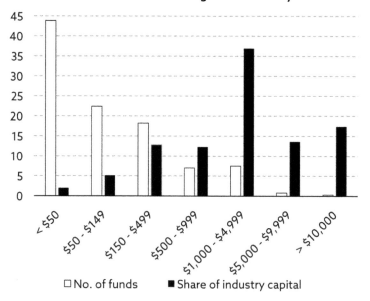

Exhibit 12.3.2: Annualised returns and volatility by fund size (AuM)

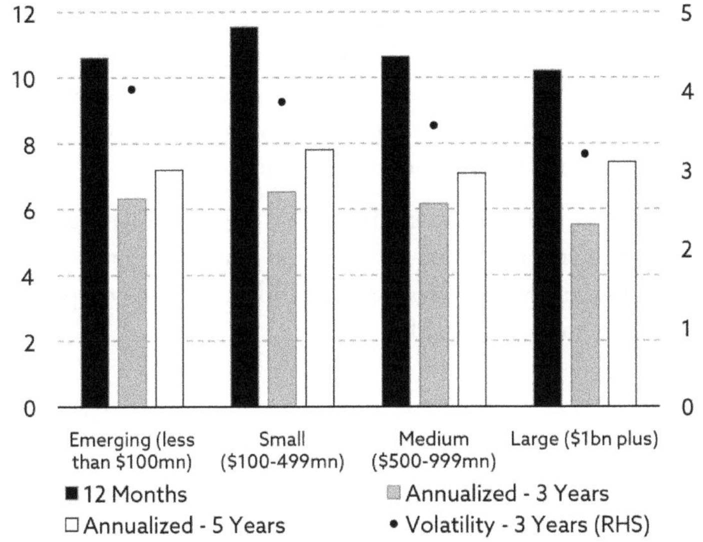

Source: Preqin (2017).

Note: Hedge funds only.

Size risk

As is evident when looking at exhibit 12.1, the size factor can have a meaningful impact on overall returns in the listed equity space but, as you can also see, the size premium is far from consistent. In some years, it is negative, whereas in other years it is positive.

However, in the illiquid (fund management) space, smaller investment managers perform better than their larger peers in most years. There are indeed many outstanding ones amongst the world's largest investment managers but, unfortunately, the best of them attract so much capital that assets under management relatively quickly become a significant hurdle. Despite that, most investors who allocate capital to external investment managers seem to think that bigger is always better.

From a practical point of view, this means that the bigger investment funds attract by far the most capital (exhibit 12.3.1), but they rarely generate the highest returns (exhibit 12.3.2), which you can take advantage of. Do not necessarily go with the smallest ones, but take advantage of the fact that there is a sweet spot in the range of $100–500 million of assets under management.[104]

Admittedly, as you can also see in exhibit 12.3.2, you have to accept modestly higher volatility for the enhanced return. On a risk-adjusted basis, the returns are not miles from each other, so it really depends on your appetite for volatility risk.

Style risk

Many investors are in love with growth stocks, and it is not difficult to understand why. Growth stocks have outperformed value stocks for many years but, if you do your homework properly, you find a close link between bond yields and the relative performance between growth and value stocks.

When bond yields decline, growth stocks outperform value stocks, and vice versa. With declining bond yields for most of the last 35 years, it is easy to understand why many investors are infatuated with growth stocks. An entire generation of investors have never seen value stocks outperform growth stocks for any extended period of time, and those who have hardly remember anymore, because it is more than 35 years ago.

Now, assuming we stand in front of a multi-year rise in interest rates, even if it is of modest proportions (as I think it will be), all that could be about to change. Moreover, if you are not comfortable assuming any beta risk at all, it would be quite easy to go long a value ETF and short a growth ETF on a risk-adjusted basis and thereby eliminate the beta risk.

---

[104] Exhibits 12.3.1–12.3.2 include hedge funds only. By not including long-only funds, am I saying they are not subject to the same dynamics? Not at all, but I don't have access to corresponding data on long-only funds.

Income risk

In the past, bonds have been the asset class of choice amongst retirees, looking for their financial portfolio to generate some much-needed income, but bonds no longer offer the income required. Consequently, the elderly seek income, wherever they can find it. That has increased the attractiveness of higher yielding equities more recently – particularly European equities, which on average offer a much higher dividend yield than US equities do.

As the ageing of the European populace will continue for at least another 30–35 years, income could be an attractive component in factor-based investing for many years to come. Likewise in the illiquid space. Expected returns on income-generating private investment strategies remain relatively attractive and continue to attract vast amounts of capital.

At the same time, that happens to be one of my biggest concerns. When capital inflows dramatically exceed the opportunity set on offer, as has been the case more recently, two things may happen. Either returns come down, or the capital is misallocated – or both. Either way, investors could end up with the short end of the stick, if they are not careful.

Illiquidity risk

Going back to the six structural mega-trends reviewed in this book, one of them is particularly guilty of driving the illiquidity premium higher, and that is *the end of the debt super-cycle*. Massive regulatory pressure on banks to reduce their loan books has led to a sub-trend I call *regulatory arbitrage*.

Banks in many countries, and particularly those in Europe, have had no choice but to offload risk. Consequently, a rising share of lending takes place away from commercial banks. Europe is still light years behind the US as far as this trend is concerned, but I expect the gap to narrow dramatically in the years to come.

In the first few years after the Global Financial Crisis erupted, a meaningful illiquidity premium existed even on relatively short-dated transactions but, nowadays, one would have to accept illiquidity for at least 3–4 years to pick up a meaningful premium.

That said, when the history books about the post-crisis environment are eventually written, one of the main topics will undoubtedly be the transformation of the lending market from commercial banks to alternative providers of credit.

A few final words

If I haven't made myself clear by now, I will spell it out so even my dog understands it.

It is time to step away from passive investing!

Investing has been *oh so simple* for the better part of the last 35 years. All you had to do was to benchmark your portfolio, and everything would take care of itself, but not anymore. For many years to come, only those who are prepared to think outside-the-box and pursue idiosyncratic investment opportunities are likely to go to bed every night with a smile on their face.

Whilst I can understand why investors are keen to move away from expensive, and notoriously underperforming, active managers, I wonder if these people understand that now is *exactly* the wrong time to go passive? The only risk factor you are exposed to when investing passively is beta risk, and that is the one risk factor you *don't* want to be overly exposed to, given the outlook laid out in this book.

Having said that, there are plenty of idiosyncratic investment opportunities up for grabs, whether you go down the alpha, credit or gamma road instead. In an unconstrained portfolio, I would allocate next to nothing to beta risk (with the possible exception of Africa), no more than 25% to alpha risk, and around 75% to credit and gamma risk.

As I have already pointed out, the gamma risk factor offering the most attractive risk premium at present is the illiquidity risk; however, it is indeed possible to combine different gamma factors. Let me give you an example. By investing in music royalties, you benefit from a significant illiquidity premium, but you also benefit from disruption (another gamma factor).

Streaming has disrupted sales of CDs, but it has also resulted in a significant increase in royalty income to the performing artist and the songwriter. Furthermore, by investing in music royalties, you receive a healthy chunk of income very regularly – much more than any decent bond is likely to offer anytime soon.

The credit risk you assume by investing in music royalties is very limited, as every (civilised) country on planet Earth has a so-called collection society, which is responsible for collecting royalties from radio and TV stations and others who play music protected under various copyright rules. In other words, you don't have to chase more than 40,000 radio stations around the world to ensure you get paid. A system is already in place worldwide.

Esoteric investment opportunities like that are much more likely to generate attractive returns for many years to come. Meanwhile, benchmark investing (indexing) has never been more popular. It continues to grow rapidly (exhibit 12.4) with over 30% of all equity capital now managed passively in North America, and it is only a question of time before more capital is managed passively than actively. According to one source[105], that will happen within a handful of years.

---

[105] Moody's (2017).

Exhibit 12.4: Flows into active versus passive investment styles (North America only)

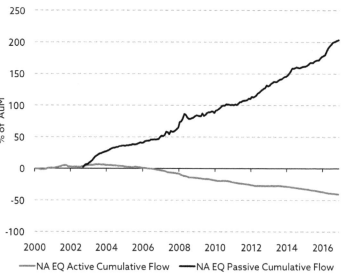

Source: EPFR Global (2017).

Note: In- and outflows are calculated on a cumulative basis and may therefore exceed 100% of AuM.

If my prediction turns out to be (broadly) accurate, there will be lots of *very* disappointed investors.

Could I be wrong?

I certainly could but, if I am, it will most likely be because (i) financial markets take a big hit relatively soon, effectively wiping the slate clean, (ii) the numerator (wealth) in the wealth-to-GDP ratio grows more slowly than the denominator (GDP) for many years to come, or (iii) the scientists miraculously dream up a methodology to produce vast amounts of fusion energy at virtually no cost.

Sadly, the last one is also the least likely to unfold anytime soon. After all, it is only Christmas once a year.

Bibliography

Advisor Perspectives (2017,1)

A Perspective on Secular Bull and Bear Markets, Jill Mislinski.

www.advisorperspectives.com/dshort/updates/2017/05/01/a-perspective-on-secular-bull-and-bear-markets

Advisor Perspectives (2017,2)

Is the Stock Market Cheap? Jill Mislinski.

www.advisorperspectives.com/dshort/updates/2017/10/02/is-the-stock-market-cheap

Amerman, Daniel (2017)

The Imminent Multi-Trillion Dollar Surge in Social Security & Medicare Costs.

danielamerman.com/va/BenefitSurge.html

Arnott, Robert & Chaves, Denis (2012)

Demographic Changes, Financial Markets, and the Economy, *Financial Analysts Journal*, Vol. 68, No. 1.

Bank for International Settlements (2015,1)

Can demographics affect inflation and monetary policy? BIS Working Paper No. 485.

Bank for International Settlements (2015,2)

Why does financial sector growth crowd out real economic growth? BIS Working Paper No. 490.

Bank of America Merrill Lynch (BofAML) (2015)
Robot Revolution – Global Robot & AI Primer.

Bank of England (2011)
Quarterly Bulletin, 3rd Quarter.

Barclays Research (2014)
Equity Gilt Study 2014.

Bawerk (2017)
bawerk.net

Brock, H Woody (2012)
American Gridlock. Hoboken, N.J.: Wiley.

Bureau of Labor Statistics (2015)
Consumer expenditures vary by age.

www.bls.gov/opub/btn/volume-4/consumer-expenditures-vary-by-age.htm

Campbell, Colin & IEA (2017)
Independent research supported by data provided by the International Energy Agency.

www.iea.org

CareerBuilder (2017)
press.careerbuilder.com/2017-08-24-Living-Paycheck-to-Paycheck-is-a-Way-of-Life-for-Majority-of-U-S-Workers-According-to-New-CareerBuilder-Survey

Conference Board, The (2017)
Total Economy Database.

www.conference-board.org/data/economydatabase/

Coyle, Diane (2014)

GDP – A brief but affectionate History. Princeton University Press.

Dalio, Ray (2016)

The 75-year debt supercycle is coming to an end.

uk.businessinsider.com/ray-dalio-ft-opinion-long-term-debt-2016-1

Dent, Harry S (2014)

The demographic cliff. Collingwood, VIC: Schwartz.

Dimson, Elroy; Marsh, Paul & Staunton, Mike (2016)

Credit Suisse Global Investment Returns Yearbook 2016. Copyright © 2016 Elroy Dimson, Paul Marsh and Mike Staunton. All rights reserved.

Dimson, Elroy; Marsh, Paul & Staunton, Mike (2017,1)

Factor-Based Investing: The Long-Term Evidence. *The Journal of Portfolio Management,* Special Issue 2017. Copyright © 2017 Elroy Dimson, Paul Marsh and Mike Staunton. All rights reserved.

Dimson, Elroy; Marsh, Paul & Staunton, Mike (2017,2)

Credit Suisse Global Investment Returns Yearbook 2017. Copyright © 2017 Elroy Dimson, Paul Marsh and Mike Staunton. All rights reserved.

Economist, The (2009)

Old-age dependency ratios.

www.economist.com/node/13611235

Economist, The (2015)

Barbarians at the farm gate.

www.economist.com/news/finance-and-economics/21637379-hardy-investors-are-seeking-way-grow-their-money-barbarians-farm-gate

Economist Intelligence Unit, The (2015)

futurehrtrends.eiu.com/report-2015/profile-of-the-global-workforce-present-and-future/

EPFR Global (2017)

www.epfrglobal.com/

European Commission (2010)

Projecting future health care expenditure at European level: drivers, methodology and main results, Economic Papers 417, Bartosz Przywara.

Eurostat (2016)

Population structure and ageing.

http://ec.europa.eu/eurostat/statistics-explained/index.php/Population_structure_and_ageing

Exergy Economics (2017)

What is Exergy?

exergyeconomics.wordpress.com/exergy-economics-101/what-is-exergy/

Feldstein, Martin (2016)

Remarks at the Brookings Institution conference on productivity.

Federal Reserve (2017)

Federal Reserve Statistical Release – Financial Accounts of the United States.

www.federalreserve.gov/releases/z1/current/z1.pdf

Federal Reserve Bank of Kansas City (2000)

The P/E ratio and stock market performance

www.kansascityfed.org/Publicat/econrev/pdf/4q00shen.pdf

Federal Reserve Bank of San Francisco (2011)
Boomer Retirement: Headwinds for US Equity Markets? Economic Letter 2011-26, Zheng Liu & Mark M Spiegel.

Financial News (2013)
The collapse of Bear Stearns: Five years on.

www.fnlondon.com

Financial Times (2017)
ETFs are eating the US stock market.

www.ft.com/content/6dabad28-e19c-11e6-9645-c9357a75844a

Fitch Ratings (2017)
Most Major EEMEA Oil Exporters Still Face Pressure from Low Prices, April 2017.

www.fitchratings.com/site/pr/1021682

Fortune Magazine (2016)
Here's Why Hedge Funds Around the World Are Cutting Their Fees.

www.fortune.com/2016/09/15/hedge-fund-fees-cut

GMO (2016)
The Stock Market as Monetary Policy Junkie: Quantifying the Fed's Impact on the S&P 500.

Gollin, Douglas (2002)
Getting Income Shares Right, *Journal of Political Economy*. Vol.110, No.2 pp.458–474.

Haldane, Andrew (2015)
Drag and Drop, speech given by A. Haldane, Chief Economist of Bank of England at the BizClub in Rutland, March 2015.

Harvard Business Review (2015)

What Is Disruptive Innovation? Clayton M. Christensen, Michael E. Raynor and Rory McDonald.

Haver Analytics, Bureau of Labor Statistics, Morgan Stanley Wealth Management Investment Resources (2017)

Demographic Destiny: Are Millennials Spending Differently Than Baby Boomers? ©2017 Morgan Stanley Smith Barney LLC.

IMF (2016)

Regional Economic Outlook, Middle East and Central Asia Department.

www.imf.org/external/pubs/ft/reo/2016/mcd/eng/pdf/mreo0416st.pdf

Institute of Economic Affairs (IEA) (2016)

Infrastructure spending and economic growth.

Institute of International Finance (2017)

Global Debt Monitor, Eye-watering rise in debt levels.

International Federation of Robotics (2017)

ifr.org

JP Morgan Asset Management (2017)

Guide to the Markets®, as of March 31, 2017. Reprinted by permission of JP Morgan Asset Management (UK) Ltd., © 2017.

KevinMD.com (2010)

The cost of keeping the terminally ill alive.

www.kevinmd.com/blog/2010/12/cost-keeping-terminally-ill-alive.html

King, Mervyn (2016)

The End of Alchemy – Money, Banking and the Future of Global Banking. London: Abacus.

King's Fund (2013)
Spending on health and social care over the next 50 years, John Appleby.

MacroStrategy Partnership LLP (2017,1)
Bad returns.

MacroStrategy Partnership LLP (2017,2)
Life's too short, and it is about to get shorter.

MacroStrategy Partnership LLP (2017,3)
The declining balance between energy cost and value.

MacroStrategy Partnership LLP (2017,4)
Double Dutch Disease.

MacroStrategy Partnership LLP (2017,5)
The productivity tipping point.

Macrotrends (2017)
S&P 500 PE Ratio – 90 Year Historical Chart

www.macrotrends.net/2577/sp-500-pe-ratio-price-to-earnings-chart

McKinsey & Company (2013)
Disruptive technologies: Advances that will transform life, business, and the global economy. McKinsey Global Institute.

McKinsey & Company (2016,1)
Diminishing Returns: Why Investors May Need to Lower Their Expectations. McKinsey Global Institute.

McKinsey & Company (2016,2)
Poorer than their parents? Flat or falling incomes in advanced economies. McKinsey Global Institute.

Moody's (2017)

www.moodys.com/research/Moodys-Passive-investing-to-overtake-active-in-just-four-to--PR_361541

OECD (2015)

The Labour Share in G20 Economies, OECD Publishing.

OECD (2016)

OECD Pensions Outlook 2016, OECD Publishing.

Pew Research Center (2017)

Immigration Projected to Drive Growth in U.S. Working-Age Population Through at Least 2035, Pew Research Center, Washington DC (Mach 2017), © 2017.

pewresearch.org/fact-tank/2017/03/08/immigration-projected-to-drive-growth-in-u-s-working-age-population-through-at-least-2035/

PhaseCapital (2015)

The Case for Dynamic Diversification.

Preqin (2017)

Does Fund Size Affect Hedge Fund Performance?

Research Affiliates (2013)

Mind the (Expectations) Gap.

Siegel, R P (2012)

Fusion Power: Pros and Cons.

www.triplepundit.com/special/energy-options-pros-and-cons/fusion-power-pros-cons/

Strategic Economic Decisions (2016)

A Novel Microeconomic Perspective on Economic Growth, Profile no. 146.

Turner, Adair (2016)

Between Debt and the Devil. Princeton University Press.

United Nations (2014)

World Urbanization Prospects.

United Nations (2015)

Department of Economic and Social Affairs, World Population Prospects, 2015 Revision.

United Nations (2016)

HDR Report.

hdr.undp.org/en/content/labour-force-participation-rate-female-male-ratio

World Bank (2012)

Global Income Equality by the Numbers: in History and Now. Policy Research Working Paper 6259.

World Economic Forum in collaboration with McKinsey & Company (2013)

Sustainable Health Systems: Visions, Strategies, Critical Uncertainties and Scenarios.

Index

Page numbers in italics (*75*) indicate exhibits. Page numbers followed by n and a number (94n55) indicate notes at the bottom of the page.

Lightning Source UK Ltd.
Milton Keynes UK
UKHW02n1435020318
318783UK00003B/132/P